HIDDEN BEERS OF BELGIUM

WRITTEN BY
BREANDÁN KEARNEY

PHOTOGRAPHY BY
ASHLEY JOANNA

FOREWORD BY ROB TOD

LUSTER

TABLE OF CONTENTS

FOREWORD BY ROB TOD (P. 4)
INTRODUCTION (P. 6)
WHAT IS A HIDDEN BEER OF BELGIUM? (P. 10)
HOW TO USE THIS BOOK (P. 14)
KEY (P. 15)
ABOUT THE PHOTOGRAPHER AND AUTHOR (P. 16)

MORE HIDDEN BEERS (P. 222)
ACKNOWLEDGEMENTS (P. 230)
GLOSSARY (P. 232)
NOTES (P. 236)

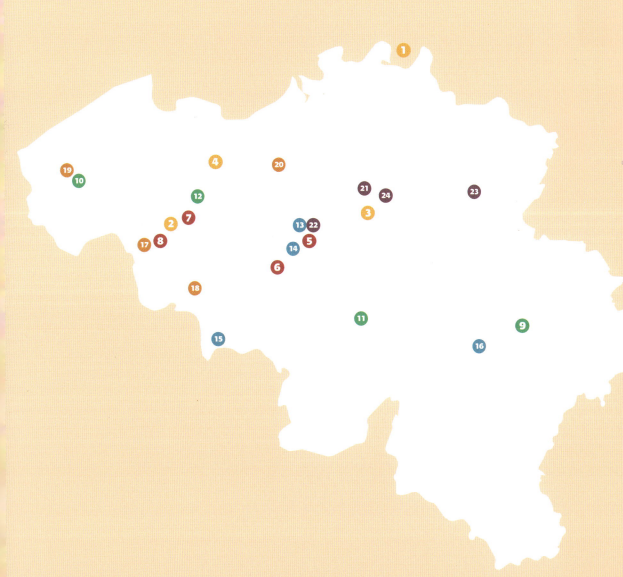

THIRST CRUSHERS

① PASSE-PARTOUT (P. 20)
Brouwerij De Dochter van de Korenaar

② SPACE CADET (P. 28)
Brouwerij 't Verzet

③ COLLEKE (P. 36)
Brouwerij de Coureur

④ PILS 13 DELTA (P. 44)
Dok Brewing Company

ACID TEST

⑤ GUEUZE HET BOERENERF (P. 54)
Het Boerenerf

⑥ OUDE QUETSCHE TILQUIN À L'ANCIENNE (P. 62)
Gueuzerie Tilquin

⑦ BIZON (P. 70)
Brouwerij Cnudde

⑧ CUVÉE FREDDY (P. 78)
Brouwerij Alvinne

WOLF PACK

⑨ HARZINGTON (P. 88)
Misery Beer Co.

⑩ KEIKOPPENBIER (P. 96)
Terrest Brewery

⑪ ELDORADO (P. 104)
Brasserie Des Champs

⑫ VALEIR EXTRA (P. 112)
Brouwerij Contreras

FUNGUS KINGDOM

⑬ BIÈRE DE TABLE (P. 122)
Brasserie La Jungle

⑭ CUVÉE DEVILLÉ (P. 130)
Brouwerij Den Herberg

⑮ LA MONEUSE (P. 138)
Brasserie de Blaugies

⑯ ARDENNE SAISON (P. 146)
Brasserie Minne

CEREAL KILLERS

⑰ FRANC BELGE (P. 156)
Brasserie De Ranke

⑱ TRIOMF (P. 164)
Brasserie Dupont

⑲ SPECIAL EXTRA EXPORT STOUT (P. 172)
De Dolle Brouwers

⑳ VICARIS WINTER (P. 180)
Brouwerij Dilewyns

UNUSUAL SUSPECTS

㉑ WHITE GOLD (P. 190)
Brouwerij Hof ten Dormaal

㉒ THÉORÈME DE L'EMPEREUR (P. 198)
Brasserie de l'Ermitage

㉓ ADELHEID (P. 206)
Brouwerij De HopHemel

㉔ DE VLIER BRUT (P. 214)
Brouwerij De Vlier

Rob Tod founded Allagash Brewing Company in 1995 with the goal of giving people new experiences with craft beer. The first beer he brewed – Allagash White – has become the most-awarded Belgian-style Witbier in the world. Under Rob's leadership, Allagash has become one of the Top 50 Craft Breweries in the U.S. (by sales volume) and has earned a spot on Maine's Best Places to Work list for ten years running. In 2021 and 2023, Allagash was also named Brewery of the Year (for its size category) at the Great American Beer Festival. Rob is the past Chair of the Brewers Association trade group and received the James Beard Award for Outstanding Wine, Beer, or Spirits Producer in 2019.

FOREWORD

It's no exaggeration to say that Belgian beer changed my life.

Before trying my first Witbier – a type of hazy, "white" ale now typically brewed with wheat, coriander, and orange peel – I had completely underestimated the range of flavours that a beer could express. It had aromas of citrus and spice. It was cloudy. It was complex yet sessionable. The experience was so powerful that it kicked off my now 30-year journey in craft brewing.

The Belgian brewing tradition is historically one of the broadest and most eclectic in the world. There are styles that are stringent in their parameters – requiring not just brewing with certain ingredients, but within a certain geographic region. And then there are styles where the guidelines are so broad as to be almost a blank slate.

But common themes do run through Belgium's beer scene: a deep reverence for the beer itself; an insistence on the need to refine and refine until the beer presents the exact intention of the brewer; and, of course, a commitment to delicious beer.

I met Breandán totally organically, through our mutual love of Belgian beers: first in 2014 at In de Verzekering tegen de Grote Dorst, a celebration of Lambics, and then a few years later at Cantillon's famed Quintessence food and beer event. He was, in his words, a young Irish guy on a journey to discover the place he now lived through the one thing in Belgium that connects its entire culture: beer. And he's been deeply rooted in that beer scene ever since, reporting on the ground for publications around the world. Ashley Joanna's photographs do an equally impressive job of placing the reader right next to the people and places that make these beers so special.

In this book, Breandán and Ashley have brought together an impressive selection of 24 beers that display the vast range of flavours available from the Belgian beer scene. From established names deepening their craft, to up-and-coming brewers expanding what Belgian beer can be, this is a book filled with new experiences for everyone – from veteran to novice beer fans.

Here's hoping you find a beer that changes your life too.

Rob Tod
Founder & Brewer
Allagash Brewing Company

INTRODUCTION

Hidden
adjective /ˈhɪdn/
"out of sight; concealed; secret."

Belgium's beers are world-famous.

You can probably list a few off the top of your head.

There are internationally known brands such as Stella Artois, Hoegaarden, and Leffe, all distributed by the world's largest brewing company: Leuven-based Anheuser-Busch InBev.

There are the Trappist ales, produced within the walls of Cistercian monasteries under the supervision of monks. Belgium is home to five of the world's 12 Trappist breweries, including the producers of iconic brands such as Orval, Westmalle, and Chimay.

Then there are the beers produced by multi-generational family breweries which have inspired enthusiasm internationally. Think of the iconic Duvel brand from the Moortgat dynasty; the Delirium Tremens range from Brouwerij Huyghe; or the powerful Bush beers of Brasserie Dubuisson.

And there are Belgium's spontaneously fermented Lambics and blended Geuzes, produced by breweries like Brasserie Cantillon and Brouwerij 3 Fonteinen, which have, in recent decades, found new international audiences.

The celebrated beers mentioned above have made Belgian beer famous around the world. But under the hood of Belgium's beer scene, beyond the big-name brands, exists a trove of breweries producing lesser-known but distinctive, varied, and extraordinary beers.

These more unfamiliar beers offer exceptional quality, diversity, and character – so much so that they've helped Belgium become the only country in the world whose beer culture is recognised by UNESCO as part of the "Cultural Heritage of Humanity."

But these hidden beers are often difficult to discover.

Firstly, there's the language barrier. Belgium has three official languages – Dutch, French, and German – but the prevalence of regional Flemish, Walloon, and East Belgian dialects means that navigating the country to find the best of its more obscure beers can be frustrating, time-consuming, and often requires local guides or translators.

Then there's Belgian beer's complex and sometimes intimidating ecosystem and nomenclature. Think of the long list of associations: the Belgian Brewers Federation; the Belgian Family Brewers; HORAL; and Zythos, among others. Abbey beers are different to Trappist beers. The terms Geuze and Oude Geuze have distinct legal protections. Something as apparently simple as the Saison style might be – because of its history, variety, and evolution – more like "a story" than a coherent beer style. It can be difficult to make sense of it all.

And then finally, there's the sheer abundance. There are estimated to be no fewer than 1,500 different beer brands available in Belgium today.

Many of the most compelling of these beers are produced by passionate people who do not have the resources to invest in promoting their products, and so they often remain confined to their regions, appreciated only by niche fandoms.

Enter *Hidden Beers of Belgium*.

This book will take you on a journey to discover the most exciting and interesting beers from Belgium which you likely never knew existed. And because a beer is never created in a vacuum, you'll learn about the remarkable places where these beers are produced, and the inspiring people who make them.

The collection of 24 beers featured between these covers is the culmination of 10 years of on-the-ground reporting and hundreds of conversations with Belgian brewers and beer professionals. This book was curated, written, and photographed completely independently, with no influence from breweries or beer industry bodies, financial or otherwise.

The beers in this book hail from Flanders, Wallonia, and the Brussels-Capital Region, evidence that different parts of the country make a rich contribution to the national beer culture.

They include many traditional Belgian styles, a reflection of the conviction and pride of Belgian brewers in maintaining the heritage of their regional specialities in the face of fast-changing markets and tastes.

But they also include modern, international styles, showcasing the creativity and versatility of brewers in Belgium, and their willingness to embrace the brewing cultures and techniques of other countries.

The beers in this book come from producers of all types. From multi-generational family breweries and from start-up brewpubs. Core beers from lesser-known brewers, and overlooked, cult beers from more famous producers.

The stories of these beers are as diverse as the beers themselves, but there are dramatic questions that unite them: How do you maintain rich family heritage while

embracing modernity and innovation? Which is more important: creative ingenuity or technical proficiency? How far should you go in pursuing your passion in the face of mounting economic challenges?

The stories in this book are about science, business, identity, war, mythology, art, history, and place. They're about relationships and love. They're about striving in the face of adversity. They're about overcoming personal tragedy.

Together, these *Hidden Beers* showcase all the reasons that Belgium is the greatest beer nation on earth.

Discover them here.

And then, go out there and find them.

WHAT IS A HIDDEN BEER OF BELGIUM?

It's a good question. When selecting the 24 beers profiled in this book, I followed these 10 simple rules.

A Hidden Beer of Belgium is:

I.
A BEER PRODUCED IN BELGIUM

Provenance means something.

It's not a criteria that the beer should be produced by Belgians. Or that it should be a traditionally Belgian style. Or that its ingredients come from Belgium. But it must be brewed, fermented, conditioned, and packaged inside the 30,688 km² that is the Kingdom of Belgium.

II.
A BEER PRODUCED BY A BREWERY OR BLENDERY

There are hundreds of Belgian beers on the market that are owned by legal entities that do not own brewing or blending facilities. They're often referred to as "contract beers".

While some of these beers are created by people working to buy their own brewing equipment, many contract beers are produced by opportunistic marketeers hoping to make a quick buck. Sometimes, they email a recipe to another facility without ever having brewed it themselves, or just put a new label on an existing beer.

Breweries and blenderies, on the other hand, are run by people who have gone all-in on their passion for beer, investing their life savings to buy equipment, working long, back-breaking hours to brew, bottle, and clean, and performing the commercial, administrative, and logistical tasks they need to survive.

I have nothing against contract beers. Many of them are excellent. A large number of their owners are passionate and highly skilled. In fact, several of the beers listed in this book were born as contract beers while their creators were building a brand, learning their trade, and fighting to secure financing for their own facilities.

But bricks-and-mortar breweries and blenderies are the lifeblood of the beer scene in Belgium. Their hidden beers are the ones I want to champion.

III.
A BEER PRODUCED BY AN INDEPENDENT BUSINESS

The beers of global brewing conglomerates in Belgium enjoy the support of well-funded and ambitious marketing professionals and vast, well-oiled distribution machines.

While many of these beers are interesting, they cannot be considered hidden.

Being independent doesn't preclude producers from being shrewd business operators or evolving with the market. Indeed, some of the beers in this book were first created by different breweries to the ones that produce them now.

I believe that while independence doesn't equate to quality, it does facilitate a courage, free-spiritedness, and self-determination that allows these producers to deliver the huge diversity of beers that make Belgian beer culture what it is.

IV.
A BEER PRODUCED ON A REGULAR BASIS

Some of the most noteworthy beers in Belgium are those produced as one-off or infrequent specials: to mark an important occasion; as part of a single collaboration; or perhaps as a seasonal experiment.

But I want you to be able to go out and try these beers for yourselves, so I've excluded ones that aren't produced on a regular basis.

Those are for another book.

V.
A BEER THAT IS READILY AVAILABLE

This book is more than a curated selection of suggestions.

It's full of beers you can actually get without having to join exclusive memberships or travel to beer festivals in remote parts of the country. You shouldn't have to slay a dragon or complete Herculean challenges to drink them.

To that end, I've included suggestions for the brewery taprooms, beer cafés, and bottle shops where you can discover each of these beers.

VI.
A BEER FROM A PRODUCER THAT HAS BEEN IN BUSINESS FOR THREE YEARS OR LONGER

Most small businesses fail within their first three years.

If you make it beyond that, then there's a good chance you'll be around for a while.

That's why every beer in this book comes from a producer that's been in business for at least three years, even if it hasn't had its own brewing facility for that long (most have been around for considerably longer). I want to be sure you'll still be able to find your hidden beers in the near future.

There are lots of great breweries and blenderies that have just started, and I look forward to including their beers in future editions.

VII.
A BEER OF HIGH QUALITY

There is no beer in this book that I do not consider to be a quality beer.

In each hidden beer, I see a standard of excellence in the raw ingredients selected, in the brewing process followed, and in the producer's commitment to delivering a unique experience.

VIII.
A BEER PRODUCED WITH KNOWLEDGE, SKILL, AND CARE

No beer worthy of inclusion here can be produced without technical expertise and knowhow.

You'd be surprised by the sheer number of decisions that go into the production of any beer, from judgements about water chemistry and mash bills to choices involving fermentation temperatures and carbonation levels for packaging.

When people understand what they're doing and have a plan, they are better placed to take risks and execute, no matter how ambitious the beer.

When they love what they do as well, the results are often spectacular.

IX.
A BEER WITH A GENUINE STORY

I appreciate good marketing. But clichés and lies obscure the authentic stories of beer.

I'm fed up with platitudes about superstar homebrewers and historical recipes that suddenly reappear.

I'm frustrated by a lack of transparency: breweries with "secret" hop varieties and "magical" yeasts.

And I'm tired of deception, as I'm sure you are. I know that the abbey on that label doesn't exist. I went there to find out. It's just a pile of ruins.

The beers in this book each tell a unique and genuine story, whether it's about the evolution of the beer scene in Belgium, the peculiarities of a particular village, or the resilience of an individual.

X.
A BEER THAT IS LARGELY UNKNOWN IN BELGIUM

The beers in this book are unlikely to be familiar to most international drinkers. And because of their hyper-regional nature and specialist distribution, they're also probably unknown to the average Belgian on the street.

Hardened beer enthusiasts may already have tasted every beer listed here. But I'm certain that the stories in this book shed new light on those same beers and will inspire enthusiasts to appreciate them in a way they perhaps hadn't before.

For Belgian beer novices, each beer listed here promises its own unique adventure.

Twenty-four adventures in total.

Savour them all.

HOW TO USE THIS BOOK

Each entry in this book gives you all the information you'll need to understand how a given beer was made, and to appreciate why it tastes the way it does. I've endeavoured to be as detailed as possible about ingredients, specifications, and processes, fact-checking as robustly as possible, but I'm ultimately bound by the willingness of producers to share details and divulge their secrets.

The contents page of this book acts as a map so you can easily navigate this landscape of hidden beers, and I've offered tips on where you're most likely to find them: brewery taprooms, beer cafés, and bottle shops.

I've included notes at the end of this book showing my reporting sources, and I've compiled a glossary of beer terms, which may be helpful for newcomers to beer.

You'll see we've capitalised beer styles, hop varieties, and the genus names of yeast and bacteria – we've done this to make the text easier to read, especially given the often-complicated nature of brewing terminology and the multifarious quality of Belgian culture and language.

Despite my attempts to select beers with staying power, it's possible that some of the beers in this book, for any number of reasons, may not be around in a few years. It's also possible that labels and packaging will change, and that beers won't appear as they do in our photographs. I'd advise that you check with breweries, shops, or cafés before visiting.

It's obvious, but it needs to be stated: Beer contains alcohol, a depressant substance associated with a range of harmful physical and mental health effects – it's worth being mindful of your alcohol consumption.

For those who choose to drink, this book will help you select beers that are high in quality, with more interesting flavour profiles, and produced by people with stories worth telling. For readers who choose not to consume alcohol, the places these hidden beers live, and the people you'll meet there, are worth the journey regardless.

So bring this book with you to bottle shops and beer cafés.

Throw it in the backseat of your car so you can plan brewery visits across Belgium.

Put it on your coffee table and let it inspire your next trip.

See if your experiences of these beers change after you've discovered their hidden stories.

KEY

ABV
Alcohol by volume
(see glossary)

IBU
International Bitterness Units
(see glossary)

EBC
European Brewing Convention,
a scale to measure the colour
intensity of a beer
(see glossary)

INGREDIENTS

Details of the water used
to brew the beer

Details of the grains used
to brew the beer

Details of the hop varieties used
in brewing the beer

Details of the yeast or bacteria
that fermented the beer

Details of the maturation process
of the beer

Details of fruit or vegetables used
in production of the beer

Details of the spices,
herbs, or flowers used as
a flavouring component

Details of any sugar added
to the beer (for colour, flavour,
or fermentation)

Details of any enzymes used
in production of the beer

Details of ingredients infused
into the beer

CYCLOPS TASTING CHART

The appearance of the beer,
with details of its colour and head

The aromas of the beer

The flavour and mouthfeel
of the beer

DISCOVER

At the brewery

From a beer café

From a bottle shop

ABOUT

THE PHOTOGRAPHER
ASHLEY JOANNA

Ashley Joanna is a photographer from New York. She possesses a talent for capturing people's portraits, fed by a genuine interest in their stories. Her portfolio includes subjects ranging from renowned chefs and athletes to artists and indigenous tribes.

Ashley's photography has been showcased worldwide as part of campaign launches for Olympus Cameras. Additionally, she has received several awards from the British Guild of Beer Writers, including the Best New Beer Writer award, for her project titled "Humans of Belgian Beer," written for *Belgian Smaak*. This project combines photography and storytelling, shedding light on individuals within the Belgian beer industry.

In her most recent ongoing project, "Menschen aus Ostbelgien," she learns about the culture of German-speaking East Belgium by taking photos and sharing stories of local people. This project has been exhibited in Brussels, Sankt Vith, and Atlanta, Georgia, and showcases the interesting lives and traditions of people from the region.

THE AUTHOR
BREANDÁN KEARNEY

Breandán is a writer from Ireland who now lives in Belgium with his Flemish wife and two young children. He is the Editor-in-Chief of the website and podcast *Belgian Smaak*.

He has written for *Lonely Planet*, *National Geographic Traveller (Food)*, *The Brussels Times*, *Parliament*, *Craft Beer and Brewing*, *Good Beer Hunting*, *Pellicle*, and *Ferment*. He is a BJCP Judge, an accredited Beer Sommelier (UK Institute of Brewing & Distilling), and a Certified Cicerone.

Breandán has been recognised as Beer Writer of the Year by both the British Guild of Beer Writers and the Irish Guild of Food Writers, and he was named Beverage Columnist of the Year by the International Association of Culinary Professionals in New York. He has won several awards for his international reporting from the North American Guild of Beer Writers, and his podcast, *Belgian Smaak*, was awarded the Best Culture Podcast at the Belgian Podcast Awards.

Thirst-quenching. Crushable. Low in alcohol
and high in drinkability. These are the *hidden beers*
that are finished before they're started.

THIRST CRUSHERS

PASSE-PARTOUT

A gluten-free Session IPA dominated by citrus, tropical fruit, and pine aromatics and flavours

Gluten-Free Session IPA
3% ABV

BROUWERIJ DE DOCHTER VAN DE KORENAAR
Oordeelstraat 3B
2387 Baarle-Hertog

IBU: 38
EBC: 30

Pale amber with a foamy, white head

Orange, apricots, lemon zest, pine, and grapefruit

Notes of caramel, citrus, and flowers, with a firm bitterness in the finish

INGREDIENTS

Baarle municipal water

Pilsner malt, Pale Ale malt, Munich malt

Southern Cross, Saaz, Amarillo, Green Bullet, Cascade, Citra, Nelson Sauvin, Simcoe, Idaho 7

American ale yeast

Enzyme to cleave gluten proteins

DISCOVER

BROUWERIJ DE DOCHTER VAN DE KORENAAR
Oordeelstraat 3B
2387 Baarle-Hertog
(Open Friday and Saturday)

L'AMÈRE À BOIRE
Rue du Belvédère 8
1050 Ixelles

DRANKEN GEERS
Ledergemstraat 7
9041 Oostakker

RECOMMENDED FOOD PAIRING

Prawn fajitas with avocado cream

ABOUT THE BREWERY

Founded: 2007
Brew capacity: 50hl
Annual production: 3,000hl

OTHER BEERS PRODUCED BY THE BREWERY

Belle-Fleur: IPA, 6% ABV

Charbon: Smoked Vanilla Stout, 7% ABV

Crime Passionnel: Wheat IPA, 7.5% ABV

Embrasse: Abbey Stout Porter, 9% ABV

Nouveau Riche: Rosemary Witbier, 6.2% ABV

OUTLIER

*In one of the most complex border areas in the world,
Ronald Mengerink of Brouwerij De Dochter van de Korenaar
strives to overcome imposed boundaries through his beers.*

I.
WIRE OF DEATH

During the First World War, the German army erected a 200km-long electric fence along the Belgian-Dutch border. The 2,000-volt Wire of Death (*Dodendraad*) separated families and friends living in frontier towns like the village of Baarle. Locals tried to dig tunnels under it or pole-vault over it. Sometimes, they would squeeze an open beer barrel under the fence and crawl through without touching the wires.

The fence is long gone, but Baarle remains one of the most complex border areas in the world. It is divided into a patchwork of enclaves, with the borderline straddling farms, roads, and even houses. Today, Baarle has been split into two villages. Of its roughly 10,000 inhabitants, 3,000 live in the Belgian territory, Baarle-Hertog, and identify as Belgian, whereas 7,000 live in the Dutch territory, Baarle-Nassau, and identify as Dutch.

There's just one brewery in the combined village of Baarle today, an independent producer called De Dochter van de Korenaar, owned and operated by Ronald Mengerink and his family. "It means beer," says Mengerink of the brewery's name, a reference to a story he discovered about Emperor Charles V preferring the juice of "the daughter of the ear of barleycorn" more than the blood of grapes.

Much like Baarle, Mengerink defies categorisation. He is a Dutchman who brews in a Belgian enclave. His beers have French names. Many are brewed with American yeast. They don't fit any particular mould. He makes hoppy session beers; classic Belgian ales; and high-ABV, barrel-aged experiments. He does so in a village that defies cartographic sense. He's been a chef, a seller of olives, a cheesemonger, and a builder of swimming pools. Today, he's a brewer who merges disparate influences into something distinctly his own.

II.
ENCLAVE

"An enclave is a piece of independent country in another independent country, completely surrounded by that country," explains Willem van Gool, chairman of Baarle's tourism office. There are only 64 enclaves in the world, and 30 of them are in the Baarle area – 22 Belgian enclaves inside the Netherlands and eight Dutch meta-enclaves inside those. This unconventional arrangement dates back to the feudal land agreements of the Middle Ages.

Baarle has, in the past, attracted those who wish to evade the authorities: a border-hopping pirate radio station; a money-laundering bank; smugglers of butter, sugar, gin, beer, and cattle. Belgian restaurants have been known to move tables across the border to take advantage of the more lax closing times in the Netherlands. Baarle has two councils, two police forces, and two fire brigades. Frans de Bont, the Belgian mayor of Baarle-Hertog, compares it to a marriage, but one in which there's no possibility of divorce. "We are condemned to each other," says de Bont. "We want to be condemned."

Mengerink found Baarle, with its fluid identity, to be the perfect environment in which to experiment. Rien Ne Va Plus is a 19% ABV American Barleywine aged in port barrels. L'Ensemble is a full malt Barleywine

> "Passe-Partout is a card that gets you anywhere. You can enter any place."
>
> — RONALD MENGERINK,
> BROUWERIJ DE DOCHTER VAN DE KORENAAR

of 13% ABV, fermented with both beer and wine yeast. Charbon is a Dry Stout of 7% ABV, brewed with smoked wheat malt and fresh vanilla. "What is in his head, he makes," says van Gool.

Mengerink's gluten-free Session IPA, Passe-Partout, is brewed with Pilsner, Pale Ale, and Munich malt, fermented with a neutral but attenuative American ale yeast, and hopped with nine varieties, from both the Old World and New, that endow it with sweet citrus, zesty grapefruit, pine, and spice aromatics and flavours. In deploying an enzyme that removes gluten from the beer, Mengerink ensures those with gluten sensitivities can enjoy it, while its relatively low ABV makes it accessible to drinkers who are moderating their alcohol consumption.

In this way, the fittingly named Passe-Partout is accessible to a broader audience of beer lovers. *Passe-partout* is a French term that refers to a master key, one that opens any lock and helps its holder cross boundaries that would not normally be passable. "Passe-Partout is a card that gets you anywhere," says Mengerink. "You can enter any place."

III.
THE FRONT-DOOR RULE

Ronald Mengerink moved to Baarle after the commercial collapse of his first brewery, De Noorderzon, in the Dutch city of Groningen. In between, he had renovated a holiday home in France and sold it with a small mark-up to raise capital for his new brewery, De Dochter van de Korenaar.

In Baarle, he found a place first on Pastoor de Katerstraat – a 500m street cut through by the international border on three separate occasions. The small house number plaque showed a Belgian flag, indicating that his address was in Belgium, not the Netherlands. In Baarle, a "front-door rule" (*voordeurregel*) determines in which country a house is located by where its front door lies. Several buildings are split in two by the border. One particular Dutch house has only its toilet in Belgium.

The national boundaries were only finalised on maps in 1995. Famously, an 84-year-old Belgian woman woke up and discovered that the border had moved a few feet to the south, and that her front door was now in the Netherlands. A proud Belgian, her solution was to swap the door with the window on its left, effectively moving the house back into Belgium.

In 2014, Mengerink moved the brewery 2km south to Baarle's Gierlestraat, doubling its capacity. Then, in 2017, he bought a farmhouse in Oordeelstraat, enabling him to brew up to 50 hectolitres at a time. It's the only building on his road that is on a Belgian plot. Even within the small confines of its own street, De Dochter van de Korenaar stands out.

IV.

MASTER KEY

Every year in September, Baarle-Hertog and Baarle-Nassau come together to celebrate the Hop over de Grens (Hop over the Border) beer festival, a charity initiative that sees brewers from both countries set up stalls on the borderline and sell their beer. Belgian and Dutch people mix together, enjoying each other's company, sharing conversation and ideas.

Just as Baarle locals once used wooden beer barrels to cross the Wire of Death, today – through initiatives such as Hop over de Grens – the beer barrel is still being used to evade borders.

Ronald Mengerink and his brewery are living proof that you don't need to accept boundaries and limitations imposed by others. You don't need to stop at the fence. You can go under it, around it, through it. You can hop over it. You can make your own all-access card, your own *passe-partout*. You can try things. You can fail. You can fail better. And in the process, you might experience something beautiful.

THIRST CRUSHERS

SPACE CADET

A zesty and refreshing wheat beer with a creamy mouthfeel and a fruity, spicy character

Witbier 5% ABV	**BROUWERIJ 'T VERZET** Grote Leiestraat 117 8570 Anzegem	IBU: 36 EBC: 7

 A pale, hazy beer with ice-cream foam

 Tangerine, stone fruits, and white pepper

 Lemon-lime-orange fruitiness with a soft mouthfeel and spicy finish

INGREDIENTS

Anzegem municipal water, adjusted to desired hardness

Pilsner malt, unmalted wheat

Magnum, Pacifica, Wai-iti

Witbier yeast

RECOMMENDED FOOD PAIRING

Cod fillet with honey lemon butter sauce

DISCOVER

BROUWERIJ 'T VERZET
Grote Leiestraat 117
8570 Anzegem

'T KRUISKE
Wafelstraat 1
8540 Deerlijk

DRANKCENTER SCHOTTE
Biesstraat 6
8790 Waregem

ABOUT THE BREWERY

Founded: 2011 as cuckoo brewers; 2016 with own brewery
Brew capacity: 20hl
Annual production: 2,500hl

OTHER BEERS PRODUCED BY THE BREWERY

Rebel Local: Hoppy Tripel, 8% ABV

Golden Tricky: Belgian IPA, 7.5% ABV

Super NoAH: Hoppy Blonde Ale, 4.9% ABV

Moose Blues: Maple Syrup Dubbel, 7.5% ABV

Oud Bruin: Oud Bruin, 6% ABV

SINGING A DIFFERENT TUNE

*Alex Lippens and his colleagues at Brouwerij 't Verzet
see themselves as underdogs. But little guys can still stand out,
experiment, and create something distinct.*

I.
UNDERDOGS

*I stand alone on the cliffs of the world
No one ever tends to me
Sitting alone, covered in rays
Some things are so my mind can breathe*

So go the lyrics to the song "Space Cadet," much loved by Alex Lippens, Koen Van Lancker, and Jens Tack – the owners of Brouwerij 't Verzet (The Resistance Brewery). The song is from the 1994 album "Welcome to Sky Valley" by Kyuss, a '90s rock band from Palm Desert in California whose music Tack describes as "stoner rock," Van Lancker as "really raw," and Lippens as "like a mental trip without using drugs."

It's a hypnotically rhythmic song with an acoustic bass riff accompanied by naked percussion – at once mellow, psychedelic, and eerie. Its abstract but thought-provoking lyrics are about feeling isolated from the world. There's a sense that the singer knows his isolation is self-imposed. He is a "space cadet" – a daydreamer who is disconnected from the reality around him.

'T Verzet's founders are space cadets. To promote their most recent six-pack offer, the three stripped down to speedos and posed as bodybuilders covered in fake tans. In various campaigns, Alex Lippens has dressed up as a Stormtrooper; an Easter bunny; a 1980s fitness guru; Jesus Christ with a crown of hops rather than thorns; and a banjo-playing, dungaree-wearing chimpanzee. "We want to be different," says Lippens.

The brewers met in the same biochemistry and brewing science course. After graduation, they went on to work for different, larger commercial breweries. In between, they produced and packaged their own 't Verzet brands at four different brewing facilities in Flanders. Eventually, after five years of building a market for their beers, they set up their own 20hl brewery in Anzegem in 2016.

"We have an underdog syndrome," says Lippens, which is reflected in their affection for what they call "underdog beer styles." Their line-up includes a "Hydro IPA" diluted with sterile hop water to lower its strength, a Ginger IPA, a Maple Syrup Dubbel, an Oud Bruin infused with oak leaves, and a hybrid Oud Bruin and Russian Imperial Stout. By being different, the three feel they can take Belgian beer to new places and add value to the community. "We try not to think in boxes," adds Van Lancker.

II.
NOSTALGIA

'T Verzet's founders believe that one of the most underdog styles of beer in Belgium today is Witbier, a pale, hazy ale brewed using high proportions of raw wheat.

The addition of wheat gives Witbiers a zesty, refreshing quality, creamy mouthfeel, and a stable, mousse-like head. The word *wit* in Flemish translates to "white," a nod to the style's signature cloudiness created by wheat proteins, polyphenols, and starch, which stay suspended in the beer.

Beers with high proportions of wheat were popular in Belgium in the 19th century, particularly in Flemish

> "Deciding to make a Witbier was a form of nostalgia."
>
> — KOEN VAN LANCKER,
> BROUWERIJ 'T VERZET

Brabant, where raw wheat was cheaper to source than malted grains. These historical Witbiers were consumed very fresh, with a herbal profile resulting from mashing with the wheat's fibrous rootlets intact. With the style's ubiquity came variety: Some versions were boiled longer, yielding a darker appearance and honey-like notes. Often, they were spontaneously fermented in wooden coolships with natural acidification by lactic acid bacteria.

Those descriptions will likely surprise contemporary drinkers. Modern Witbiers are generally modelled on Hoegaarden, the beer originally created in 1966 by Belgian milkman Pierre Celis. Celis spiced the beer with bitter orange peel and coriander, but he also reputedly deployed chamomile to add a delicate floral note. When Anheuser-Busch InBev, then Interbrew, bought Celis' brewery in 1989, other breweries in Belgium took note of Hoegaarden's commercial success and created their own versions.

Over the years, commercial Witbiers became thinner in body, more heavily spiced, and sweeter. In the 2000s, Witbier's popularity in Belgium began to decline, eclipsed by other styles such as European Pale Lager and Strong Belgian Ales. "It disappeared," says Van Lancker. "It's a shame because it's a great style."

Lippens and Van Lancker say they remember their uncles drinking Witbier in the 1990s and they lament the ways it's become less popular in the years since. "Deciding to make a Witbier was a form of nostalgia," says Van Lancker. "We wanted to bring it to life again, but in our different way."

III.
HEROES

In 't Verzet's barrel room, each of the 107 barrels and four foeders for maturing mixed-fermentation beer is dedicated to a pioneering musician, their names scribbled in chalk on the oak.

There are "punk rock" barrels named after Kurt Cobain, Iggy Pop, and Patti Smith; "blues" barrels named for PJ Harvey, Rory Gallagher, and B.B. King; and hip-hop barrels named for Lauryn Hill, Busta Rhymes, and Tupac. "They're our heroes," says Van Lancker.

Two of the barrels are also named for John Garcia and Josh Homme, the former singer-songwriter and guitarist of Kyuss. "They're also underdogs," says Lippens

of Kyuss. "I think the band really appealed to us because of their standing in society."

The three decided to brew a new Witbier every year, each named after a different Kyuss song. To make their Witbier distinct from other commercial versions of the style, they aimed to recreate the flavours of coriander and bitter orange peel without using those ingredients. They selected a yeast with a spicy, phenolic character and chose Belgian Cascade and New Zealand Rakau hops to accentuate the beer's citrus notes. They wanted to be loyal to Celis' example of playing with Witbier's fruitiness and spiciness, but to "do it in a different way," according to Van Lancker. "We wanted to add some balls to it."

> "We have an underdog syndrome."
>
> — ALEX LIPPENS,
> BROUWERIJ 'T VERZET

IV.
GREEN MACHINE

The beer they released in 2017 was named after the Kyuss song "Green Machine." However, the small batch was produced in keg only, and bars and restaurants refused to order the beer unless they could try samples in bottle. The following year, 't Verzet's owners didn't make the same mistake.

Not only did they brew a bigger batch of Witbier and package it in both kegs and bottles, they tweaked the recipe to improve it, changing the hop varieties. They opted for Belgian Magnum for bittering because of its subtle citrus flavours, and two New Zealand varieties for late and dry hopping: Pacifica for its spice and orange notes, and Wai-iti for its lime and stone fruit character. A new Witbier. A new Kyuss-inspired name.

So popular was Space Cadet when it was released in 2018 that brewery co-owner and sales manager Jens Tack convinced Lippens and Van Lancker not to change the recipe any further. "It was added value to the market because there weren't a lot of wheat beers at that time," says Tack. They stopped brewing new Witbiers themed on Kyuss songs and moved Space Cadet into their year-round core range.

The space cadets at 't Verzet do what they want, often disconnected from the wider brewing landscape. They fight for the underdog and celebrate uniqueness. The space cadet knows he's different. He feels it's necessary to be so. This is the only way his mind can breathe.

COLLEKE

A clean, crisp, and easy-drinking ale produced by a cycling-themed neighbourhood brewery in a cosy Leuven suburb

Cream Ale 4.5% ABV	**BROUWERIJ DE COUREUR** Borstelsstraat 20/bus 1 3010 Kessel-Lo (Leuven)	IBU: 14 EBC: 9
 Pale straw with a fluffy white head	 A sweet, crackery, almost corn-like aroma, with subtly floral hoppy notes	 Grainy and dry with a bitter, refreshing finish

INGREDIENTS

Kessel-Lo municipal water

Pilsner malt, rice flakes, corn flakes

Belgian Goldings

English ale yeast

RECOMMENDED FOOD PAIRING

Barbecue pork with jalapeño salsa

DISCOVER

BROUWERIJ DE COUREUR
Borstelsstraat 20/bus 1
3010 Kessel-Lo (Leuven)
(Always on tap)

MALZ
Brusselsestraat 51
3000 Leuven
(Sometimes on tap)

HOPS 'N MORE
Parijsstraat 27
3000 Leuven
(Sometimes on the shop's tap)

ABOUT THE BREWERY

Founded: 2020
Brew capacity: 4.5hl
Annual production: 100hl

OTHER BEERS PRODUCED BY THE BREWERY

Souplesse: Belgian Tripel, 6.9% ABV

Kuitenbijter: American IPA, 6.3% ABV

CHANGING GEARS

Colleke was conceived from a terrible bike accident and born in a devastating pandemic; it's a beer which signals hope, if you can just conquer the hill you're climbing.

I.
THE ACCIDENT

In 2014, Bart Delvaux and Ine Van der Stock boarded a plane to America.

They had met at university in Leuven, and owned a house together in the suburb of Kessel-Lo. They both loved cycling. Van der Stock worked in sustainable tourism, while Delvaux was a project manager for a software development company. When Delvaux's employer asked him to manage the relocation of its offices to Chicago, the Belgian couple found themselves moving to Illinois.

On Saturday, 18 July 2015, Delvaux went for an afternoon cycle along the shores of Lake Michigan. A group of beachgoers heading back towards the city centre absentmindedly walked across the bicycle lane. Delvaux swerved to avoid them, but he hit a stone, causing him to crash. His bike was wrecked, his cycling jersey ripped, and his body covered in blood.

He had broken his hip, and doctors were concerned that an arterial injury might lead to haemorrhage. He was rushed to an operating theatre for emergency surgery.

II.
GREENBUSH

The operation was a success, but the surgeon told Delvaux that he had been lucky. "He could have lost his leg," says Van der Stock.

The couple had hoped to spend their summer hiking in Alaska, but they couldn't venture far until Delvaux recovered. Instead, they went on a day trip to Sawyer, a quaint lakeside town located at Michigan's southwestern tip, less than two hours from Chicago by car. Van der Stock drove them; once they arrived, Delvaux hobbled everywhere on crutches.

Feeling peckish, they popped into a local brewpub, Greenbush Brewing. It was different to the beer cafés they had frequented in Belgium. They saw executives in suits sitting beside waste disposal workers, enjoying great food together and sharing fresh draught beer that was produced only metres away. "It was an amazing atmosphere," says Delvaux.

The discovery of taproom culture in the U.S. sparked a series of trips all over the country. "In total, I visited breweries in 49 states," says Delvaux.

On one of those trips, he and Van der Stock discovered Cream Ale: a clean, refreshing, top-fermented ale, first produced by American brewers in the mid 1800s to compete with the influx of European lagers. The "cream" in its name didn't refer to any dairy products, but to its purported rich, silky, and smooth mouthfeel. "It's what the Americans call 'a lawnmower beer,'" says Delvaux of the thirst-quenching ale. The Belgian couple loved it, and their new life in the U.S.

Or at least they did until 8 November 2016, when Donald J. Trump was elected as the 45th President of the United States. Trump fuelled controversy with his views on race and immigration, incidents of violence at his rallies, and numerous sexual misconduct allegations. "Chicago all of a sudden had really negative energy and lots of demonstrations," says Van der Stock.

> "It's what the Americans call 'a lawnmower beer.'"
>
> — BART DELVAUX,
> BROUWERIJ DE COUREUR

For the first time, the couple started talking about the possibility of going home. Inspired by their experiences in taprooms across the U.S., they had the idea of opening a small brewery and taproom back in Kessel-Lo. The Leuven suburb had become a lively and highly desirable home for professionals, creatives, and young families. Its disused spaces had become recreational parks, its old industrial buildings transformed into food halls and sports centres.

If there were a place in Belgium for Delvaux and Van der Stock to open a neighbourhood taproom, it had to be in Kessel-Lo.

III.
SMALL HILL

Delvaux and Van der Stock found an old Renault car workshop in Kessel-Lo which dated back to 1927. Its spacious atrium led into a long, high-ceilinged warehouse. They set up a two-kettle brewery system with four 5hl fermentation vessels and installed three horizontal serving tanks in the taproom so they could pour fresh beer on draught, brewed and packaged fewer than 10 metres away. They planned to open in the spring of 2020.

They named their brewery for the *coureur* – "rider" in cycling speak. "We wanted to turn the negative experience into something positive," says Delvaux of his Chicago bike accident. It was to be an ode to two of Belgium's most iconic pastimes: beer and bikes. The couple hoped people would cycle to their brewery, whether it was families on longtails and cargo bikes, recreational cyclists taking a break from the hills around Leuven, or those drawn to the city by its international cycling tournaments.

Their first beer was Colleke, a 4.5% ABV Cream Ale, produced with Pilsner malt and small amounts of rice and corn flakes to lighten the body. Delvaux and Van der Stock fermented the beer with a subtle English ale yeast, and hopped it with Belgian Goldings for a classic, delicate finish. *Colleke* means "small hill." "When you've just climbed a small hill on your bike, you need a refreshing beer," says Delvaux.

Then, the COVID-19 pandemic hit. Brouwerij de Coureur was prohibited from opening by the Belgian government. The ride was nearly over before it had begun.

IV.
DOWNHILL

Bart Delvaux and Ine Van der Stock clung to their dream and spent the pandemic brewing beer and decorating their unopened taproom. Their IPA was named *Kuitenbijter* (literally "calf biter," a nasty hill which burns your calves) and their Tripel *Souplesse* (riding *op souplesse* means to ride "effortlessly"). They based their logo on an illustration by their nine-year-old niece Lilia, a top-down view of a cyclist in full flow.

Meanwhile, they secured cycling paraphernalia from their local bike shop: antique bikes, unique saddles, and strange wheels. They put up a series of old French cycling magazine articles on the wall of their back office. In the taproom, they mounted a line-up of handlebars on the wall like the trophy antlers of hunted animals.

When the government finally allowed hospitality businesses to reopen on 8 June 2020, De Coureur was ready to offer a neighbourhood taproom experience. Visitors enjoyed its tasting flights of beers, known, in the brewery's parlance, as *pelotons*. Patrons sat on repurposed bike-saddle barstools. The brewery even hung repair tools from the wall, so customers could fix their bikes between drinks.

Delvaux and Van der Stock have continued to put in place initiatives that have embedded the brewery into the fabric of Kessel-Lo life. They've provided games for children to play and tricycles for them to ride, ensuring the space is family-friendly; they've donated to local charity projects. They've learned their patrons' names. They've learned their patrons' dogs' names.

They also established a "pay-it-forward" scheme, which encourages visitors to buy a beer or set aside an amount of money, no matter how small, for friends (or strangers) to spend at the taproom. At any given time, there are between 20 and 30 prepaid cards attached to a board beside the bar.

The success of Brouwerij de Coureur is no accident. The brewery's founders set their sights on a hill to climb, and they conquered it. When their patrons visit, they start with Colleke, so they too can freewheel downhill from whatever summit they've climbed that day.

PILS 13 DELTA

*A dry, thirst-quenching lager with a balanced body,
earthy hop character, and refreshing finish*

Pilsner
4% ABV

DOK BREWING COMPANY
Dok-Noord 4B
9000 Ghent

IBU: 55
EBC: 6

Pale gold with
a long-lasting white head

Grainy, herbal,
and earthy

Biscuity malt with
a bitter, spicy hop finish

INGREDIENTS

Ghent municipal water

Pilsner malt

Hallertau Mittelfrüh,
Saaz, Magnum

Lager strain with a neutral
fermentation profile

RECOMMENDED FOOD PAIRING

Gourmet hamburger from
RØK Barbecue & Burgers

DISCOVER

DOK BREWING COMPANY
Dok-Noord 4B
9000 Ghent

CAFÉ DE WELKOM
Oudburg 70a
9000 Ghent

DE HOPDUVEL
Dok-Noord 7/bus 05
9000 Ghent

ABOUT THE BREWERY

Founded: 2018
Brew capacity: 20hl
Annual production: 1,000hl

**OTHER BEERS PRODUCED
BY THE BREWERY**

Waar is Loca: Belgian Pale Ale,
6.5% ABV

AUTHENTIC

*If at first you don't succeed, try and try again.
Pilsner is the most popular and competitive beer segment in Belgium,
but when Dimitri Messiaen couldn't find one with the character
he wanted, he kept brewing until he did.*

I.
LOADING DOK

Dimitri Messiaen – hair styled in a greying, trendy undercut; wearing dark, thick-rimmed glasses; and showcasing a carefully kempt handlebar moustache – is a creative entrepreneur in Belgium's food and drinks scene. He co-created Pils 13, a beer brand now produced by Dok Brewing Company, which he co-owns with Janos De Baets; Koen Van Laere; and his son, Arthur Messiaen.

Messiaen has spent years working in cafés, restaurants, and drinks distributors. For nearly as long, he was on the hunt for a characterful Pilsner to sell with food. He sought a beer that wasn't a copy of mass-produced industrial lagers, many of which deploy cheap ingredients to keep costs down, shorten production times to increase volume, and subdue hop character to appeal to as wide a market as possible.

For Messiaen, Pilsner wasn't just a beer. It was a critical core offering for any café or restaurant, a statement to the consumer about the type of business you were

> "If you eat always a Dr. Oetker pizza, you don't know how a fresh pizza tastes."
>
> — DIMITRI MESSIAEN,
> DOK BREWING COMPANY

running. He wanted a Pilsner that was authentic, not dumbed-down. But while he found it easy to curate high-quality wine lists for his restaurants and source fresh, local ingredients for his kitchens, he had a much harder time finding the Pilsner that would help him show Belgians what Pilsner could be.

II.
CHARACTER

Despite Belgium's storied reputation for strong, abbey-style ales and regional mixed- and spontaneous-fermentation specialities such as Lambic and Oud Bruin, it is Pilsner – or a prevailingly bland interpretation with low levels of maltiness and hop bitterness, sometimes described as "International Pale Lager" – that is the most popular beer style in the country.

Many versions are brewed using adjuncts, such as corn or rice, as opposed to a full grain bill of malted barley. They're filtered and pasteurised to kill biological activity and aid shelf stability, rather than presented as living drinks with their full range of flavour compounds intact. In many cases, hop extracts are used rather than hops themselves. Production time can be as little as a week compared to the sometimes months-long conditioning of traditional Pilsners. The results are easy-drinking and sometimes slightly sweet, with very little character.

Messiaen contacted smaller independent breweries to ask if they could make a characterful Pilsner he could sell. "Nobody did it," he says. He soon discovered why.

Beer cafés in Belgium are generally owned by regional or international breweries, and so it is very difficult to distribute outside of this network. It's also difficult to compete on margin with mass-market Pilsners, given the economies of scale enjoyed by larger players and the expectations among Belgian drinkers of low price points.

But perhaps the biggest challenge in sourcing a more characterful Pilsner was that Belgians were used to drinking soft, slightly sweet, and less hoppy Pilsners. "It's like if you eat only McDonald's burgers, you don't know how a non-industrial burger tastes," says Messiaen. "If you eat always a Dr. Oetker pizza, you don't know how a fresh pizza tastes."

If no one else would make one, Messiaen would do it himself.

III.
ITERATIONS

Pilsner originates from the Czech city of Pilsen, where brewers combined lagering periods of several months and a new kind of yeast that fermented at colder temperatures with their own soft water, pale malt, and Saaz hops. Czech-style Pilsner today tends to have a rich, full mouthfeel and body due to the traditional decoction mashing technique, in which part of the mash is boiled separately, and then returned to the main mash. German-style Pilsner, on the other hand, typically features more minerality in the brewing water, domestic German hop varieties, and very clean fermentations. These Pilsners tend to be more dry, bitter, hop-forward, and crisp.

Dimitri Messiaen began homebrewing Pilsner in his kitchen with his childhood friend Koen Van Laere. He approached it as a chef making soup. "Our product was not good enough," says Messiaen, so the pair went to brewing school, and for two years, brewed different versions of their Pilsner – each one iterating on the last – in a cycle of continuous improvement and learning.

After every iteration, Messiaen and Van Laere asked friends and beer enthusiasts to try their beer. Less-experienced drinkers often didn't like it. But with the 13th iteration of their Pilsner, their friends suggested that the beer was too good for Messiaen and Van Laere to have brewed it themselves. "That's when I said, 'Okay, we have something special,'" says Messiaen.

Their favoured recipe combined the biscuity malt notes and spicy Saaz character of the Czech-style Pilsner with the pronounced bitterness and subtle citrus hop character associated with the German-style Pilsner. They dry-hopped the beer with Hallertau Mittelfrüh for an added herbal, floral, and woody aroma. To facilitate colloidal drop-out and dissipate unwanted compounds, they gave each batch a long conditioning time at cold temperatures, typically around two-and-a-half months before packaging.

Before Dok, they didn't have a brewery of their own, so they produced the first commercial batch as The Ministry of Belgian Beer in 2015 at Brouwerij Contreras in Gavere, a production run of 6,000 litres. For an unknown brand, it was a lot of beer. Messiaen and Van Laere sold it within a month.

IV.
DELTA VARIANT

Today at Dok, you can try a variety of Pils 13 variants alongside Arthur Messiaen's smoked meat offerings from RØK Barbecue & Burgers. There's a dry-hopped 13, a Green-Hop 13, an Export 13, and even a Black Lager 13.

The bottled versions are still brewed at Contreras, while the canned and draught versions are produced at Dok. Both versions are fermented with lager yeast sourced from Contreras and now propagated for Dok by KU Leuven. Messiaen likes to stress that there's a difference between the beers produced at Contreras and at Dok, given their distinct brewing set-ups. As a result, the canned version carries a Delta symbol, a scientific indication that there's a change in one variable.

While Dok's entire lager line is now branded with 13, Messiaen didn't always think using the number was the best choice because of its unlucky connotations.

At one point in the early days – after reading about successful beer brand launches and speaking with marketing professionals – Messiaen visited the archives of the Museum of Fine Arts in Ghent. He was looking for a recipe from yesteryear similar to his own, with a name that might resonate with consumers.

But while among the archives, he had a realisation.

"I was in there and said, 'What am I doing?'" he says. "I'm lying to myself."

He had been lamenting the absence of an authentic Pilsner in Belgium, and now he was on the verge of adopting that same inauthenticity by cherry-picking a historical brand and fabricating a story about it.

"I'm not doing it like a lot of the rest," he said. "We call it 13, and that's it."

Wild yeast and bacteria produce a complex array of flavours in many Belgian beers. Whether it's a tangy tartness, a fruity sourness, or a puckering bite, these are the *hidden beers* that will bring zing to your life.

ACID TEST

GUEUZE HET BOERENERF

A soft and balanced spontaneous-fermentation beer with lemony acidity; white pepper spice; and a woody, dry finish

Geuze 5.5% ABV	**HET BOERENERF** Sollenberg 3 1654 Beersel	Specifications vary each year depending on Lambic used and blending considerations.
 Golden blonde, with a spritzy carbonation	 Citrus zest, green apple, and gooseberry	 Overripe lemon, white pepper, and leather, with a tart, woody-dry finish

INGREDIENTS

Senne Valley municipal water

Malted barley, raw wheat

Aged hops of various varieties

Coolship inoculation with spontaneous fermentation involving a wide range of yeast and bacteria

Ageing in oak barrels of various Lambics from 3 Fonteinen, De Troch, Angerik, Lindemans, Den Herberg, and Sako

DISCOVER

HET BOERENERF
Sollenberg 3
1654 Beersel
Open Saturday only
(from May to September)

CAFÉ 'T PARLEMENT
Klinkaert 10
1500 Halle

BIERHANDEL DEKONINCK
Felix Roggemanskaai 18
1501 Halle

RECOMMENDED FOOD PAIRING

Pork and apple stew

ABOUT THE BLENDERY

Founded: 2020
Brew capacity: 20hl
Annual production: 400hl

OTHER BEERS PRODUCED BY THE BLENDERY

Symbiose: Blend of Lambic, cider, and mead; varying ABVs

Oude Cider: Oak-aged cider blend with apple, quince, and pear; 6% ABV

Gueuze Cuvée Heritage: Geuze, 7% ABV

Zomerkriek: Blend of cherry Lambic and cider, 7% ABV

Biet: Beetroot Lambic, 7% ABV

BETTING THE FARM

Through Gueuze Het Boerenerf, Senne Eylenbosch saved his father's farm, discovered his own identity, and began the next chapter in the story of his family's Lambic heritage.

I.
ICE CREAM

Senne Eylenbosch grew up on his family's farm. His parents, organic dairy farmers Paul Eylenbosch and Veerle Samyn, produced everything from yoghurt to butter before choosing to focus on their best-selling product: ice cream. In addition to supplying local shops, they sold a variety of flavours at events such as the Kasteelfeesten, a biennial summer event at Beersel Castle.

At the 17th edition of the Kasteelfeesten, in 2011 – when Eylenbosch was 15 years old – he snuck off to the next tent, where Sidy Hanssens of Geuzestekerij Hanssens handed him a glass of Hanssens Oude Kriek. She even gave him a €5 note to buy a Kriek from another producer, so he could understand how other versions of the style tasted against "a real one." It was a small gesture that made a big impression on a young Eylenbosch.

The story of Lambic was never far away. The building next door to where he lived, now a block of apartments, was once a Lambic brewery dating back to the 1860s, owned for a period of time by members of his own bloodline.

The old farm brewery came into the Eylenbosch family when Anna Maria Cammaert married Martinus Josephus Eylenbosch in 1874, and their descendants continued production of Geuze until 1965, when the brewery closed. Senne Eylenbosch isn't sure why the family shut the brewery, but "something happened" and he says there's a sense of "shame" in the way older members of his family talk about it now. "It was a big scar in the family," he says.

The farm eventually made its way into the possession of Senne Eylenbosch's father, Paul, and it's where Eylenbosch opened Het Boerenerf in 2020.

Eylenbosch is not a brewer but a blender. He sources inoculated wort from Lambic breweries, ageing the spontaneously fermenting wheat beer in barrels to produce his own fruit blends and Geuzes. But while Eylenbosch embraces the family brewing history, he doesn't want to be tied to it. "It's four generations back," he says. "I will not take their heritage to sell my beer. I don't think it's authentic." He uses the Flemish phrase, *pluimen verdienen* (literally to "deserve your feathers"), which means to "earn kudos". But it comes out in his English translation a little differently: "I want to deserve my own plums."

II.
MENTOR

After school, Senne Eylenbosch didn't know what he wanted to do. He worked as a nature guide in the Sonian Wood near Brussels, and thought about becoming a primary school teacher. But then opportunity arose at a Lambic brewery that had just expanded nearby, and which needed extra hands. On 7 July 2016, Eylenbosch started working at Brouwerij 3 Fonteinen. "Lambic was a way of life," says Eylenbosch of 3 Fonteinen. "It was 'all-in' stuff."

There, Eylenbosch rubbed shoulders with Armand Debelder, the storied previous owner of 3 Fonteinen. Debelder was not only a respected figure in the world of Lambic, known for his work ethic, highly regarded palate, and passionate demeanour, but he was also

> "It's four generations back. I will not take their heritage to sell my beer. I don't think it's authentic. I want to deserve my own plums."
>
> — SENNE EYLENBOSCH,
> HET BOERENERF

beloved in the local community. Eylenbosch remembers Debelder dancing with his mother Veerle at the Kasteelfeesten.

On one occasion at 3 Fonteinen, inspired by older Lambics (which sometimes present a hazelnut character), Eylenbosch tried to create a Lambic with real hazelnuts. He spent hours working on the blend, and in a fit of excitement, when the Lambic was just three weeks old, brought Debelder a glass of cloudy, white haze. Eylenbosch says Debelder took the glass, looked at it, and immediately pushed it back across the table. He remembers Debelder's next words: "If you don't respect it enough to age it, I will not even taste it." Nothing ever came of this Lambic.

When Senne Eylenbosch blends, he bases his decisions on four components: bitterness, acidity, mouthfeel, and aroma. But Debelder's lesson was clear. If Eylenbosch didn't have the patience to let his beers develop, then he would never understand Lambic. He now recognised the crucial fifth component to his process: time.

III.
A MATTER OF TIME

Eylenbosch never intended to start his own blendery. He thought he might do something with beer when he was older – "When I know who I am" – but not in his 20s.

But then, in 2019, Eylenbosch's mother left the family farm after divorcing his father. She took the ice-cream business with her, and so Paul Eylenbosch had to make the farm work economically without a crucial source of revenue. There was no possibility of expansion, as the land was excluded from the appropriate zoning permits.

Senne Eylenbosch was 23 years old. Someone would have to buy out his mother's share and run a business that would make enough money to keep it going. "I'm too young," said Eylenbosch. "I don't want to take that responsibility. I don't have the money or the knowledge."

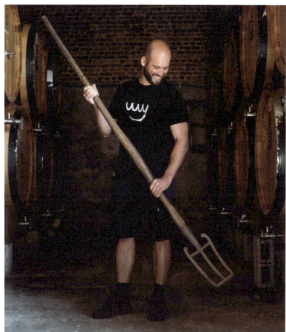

But soon he changed his mind. He talked with the leadership at 3 Fonteinen and they were supportive, so he acted fast and bought wort produced during that Lambic brewing season rather than waiting more than half a year for the next season to start. He wanted to give his Lambic the thing it needed most: time. He was able to source 10 barrels, and he filled them with wort from 3 Fonteinen. In the summer of 2020, Eylenbosch officially left 3 Fonteinen. The Zenne Valley had a new Lambic blendery.

IV.
FARMSTEAD

Initially, Eylenbosch was not keen to refer to the old farm brewery that his family had operated. "We look forward to the future," says Eylenbosch. "I'm not selling beer from a brewery which once existed. I'm from 1995. The brewery stopped in 1965. That's 30 years difference. I've never seen the brewery." But he also didn't want to totally dismiss his family heritage.

When one of Eylenbosch's relatives discovered trinkets from the old Eylenbosch farm brewery in their cellar, they asked if Eylenbosch wanted them. There was a stave from one of the foeders, complete with a metal plaque indicating its number, 478. Eylenbosch was glowing. "Of course I want to have a piece of heritage back," he said.

There were other pieces of heritage, too: wooden crates, a barrel ladder, a barrel brush, a brewing fork, glassware, and old bottles of Geuze. Eylenbosch also had the *tonmerk*, or "barrel mark," of the old brewery: a series of "U"-shaped waves, each of which, according to Eylenbosch, symbolises one generation of brewery ownership.

The *tonmerk* is now the logo of Het Boerenerf. In Flemish, *Het Boerenerf* has a double meaning. It translates directly as "The Farmstead" – Senne Eylenbosch is a farmer, just like his father, his grandfather, and his great-grandfather before him – but the word *erf* in *Boerenerf* also refers to *erfgoed*, meaning "heritage."

All of Eylenbosch's considerations and dilemmas seem to coalesce in his blendery's eponymous Geuze: respecting the heritage of the old brewery without relying on it; embracing his identity as a farmer; and producing Lambic which is innately personal but also respectful of its tradition.

OUDE QUETSCHE TILQUIN À L'ANCIENNE

A hazy pink-orange fruit Lambic with aromas of plum brandy and herbal tea; a sour, stone fruit jamminess; and a dry finish

Plum Lambic
6.4% ABV

GUEUZERIE TILQUIN
Chaussée Maïeur Habils 110
1430 Bierghes (Rebecq)

IBU: 15
EBC: N/A

Hazy orange with
a mousse-like, white head

Plum brandy, herbal tea,
red berries, and lemon zest

Oaky, acidic, fruity,
and dry

INGREDIENTS

Senne Valley municipal water

Malted barley, raw wheat

Aged hops of various varieties

Coolship inoculation with
spontaneous fermentation
involving a wide range
of yeast and bacteria

Ageing in oak barrels

French plums

DISCOVER

GUEUZERIE TILQUIN
Chaussée Maïeur Habils 110
1430 Bierghes (Rebecq)
(Open Saturday)

NÜETNIGENOUGH
Rue du Lombard 25
1000 Brussels

MALT ATTACKS
Avenue Jean Volders 18
1060 Saint-Gilles

RECOMMENDED FOOD PAIRING

Spiced plum, walnut,
and honey crumble tart

ABOUT THE BLENDERY

Founded: 2009
Blending capacity: 42hl
Annual production: 1,500hl

OTHER BEERS PRODUCED BY THE BLENDERY

Gueuze Tilquin à l'Ancienne:
Oude Geuze, 7% ABV

Oude Mûre Tilquin à l'Ancienne:
Blackberry Lambic, 6% ABV

Oude Rhubarbe Tilquin à l'Ancienne:
Rhubarb Lambic, 6% ABV

Pinot Noir Tilquin à l'Ancienne:
Pinot Noir Lambic, 8.2% ABV

Pinot Gris Tilquin à l'Ancienne:
Pinot Gris Lambic, 8.4% ABV

THE OUTSIDER

Pierre Tilquin was never supposed to be a Lambic producer.
But when you're stubborn, you can forge your own path.

I.
STATISTICIAN

Pierre Tilquin was tired of studying. He had completed a five-year degree in bioengineering for animal breeding and earned a PhD in statistical genetics. "I wanted to do something more practical," he says. That something practical, he realised after drinking Geuze in Brussels cafés, would be producing Lambic.

Lambic is a spontaneously fermented wheat beer. It can be old or young, carbonated or flat, fruited or unfruited, and sweetened or unsweetened. Different Lambics are blended into Geuze. The more Lambic he tasted, the more fascinated Tilquin became.

To facilitate his career change, Tilquin worked for more than a year at Brouwerij Huyghe in Melle, famous for its Delirium Tremens Golden Strong Ale. He then secured six-month periods of work experience at 3 Fonteinen and Cantillon, two notable producers of Lambic. "Cantillon gives you the impression that you are in a farm in the city," he says. "Not breeding animals, but breeding Lambics."

Tilquin says he learned a lot – how to taste, how to clean, and how to blend. But his demeanour was socially awkward; his communication direct; his personality singular and headstrong. "I realised with my specific character that I couldn't stay in small breweries," says Tilquin. "If I wanted to work in a Lambic blendery or brewery, I'd have to create my own."

II.
BLENDING

Tilquin is from Wallonia; the southern, French-speaking part of Belgium. All of the other Lambic producers were from the Pajottenland region or Brussels.

Many of them belonged to HORAL, the Hoge Raad voor Ambachtelijke Lambiekbieren (High Council for Traditional Lambic Beers). They held their meetings in Flemish and accepted only Pajot or Brusseleir Lambic producers as members. Importantly, HORAL also granted members access to the Toer de Geuze, a biannual event which attracted thousands of international visitors. Being an official stop on the Toer de Geuze was both culturally significant and commercially important for Lambic producers.

Unable to afford rent in Brussels, Tilquin started blending in 2009 in the Walloon village of Bierghes, 30 kilometres to the southwest of the Belgian capital. He opened a blendery, not a brewery, buying his wort from other Lambic brewers and then ageing it, blending it, and packaging it in his own style. When Tilquin opened his doors in 2011, his was the first new blendery to debut in more than a decade, and the only Walloon Lambic blendery in Belgium. He described his business as a *gueuzerie*. "Blendery is *stekerij* in Flemish," says Tilquin. "The word doesn't really exist in French. *Gueuzerie* is a good mix between *gueuze* and *brasserie*."

Tilquin brought his scientific mindset to blending. He sourced wort from five breweries: Boon, Lindemans, Girardin, Cantillon, and Timmermans. He worked according to precise and repeated ratios and kept spreadsheets of sugar content and other important fermentation parameters. "We do a lot of measurements," says Tilquin. "I have some colleagues that are blending

like artists, and it's nice, but I feel the necessity of understanding what I blend."

Tilquin's Geuze would be *malse*: soft, balanced, and well-conditioned. Without any revenue coming in for two and a half years while his Lambic matured, he managed to secure some capital from investors. But his whole future hinged on the reception of his first beers. In order to start with a bang, he decided to blend a fruit beer, but not with the traditional fruits used in Lambic – sour cherries (*krieken*) and raspberries (*frambozen*). "My idea was to produce something else," he says.

III.
PLUM JOB

After some trials, Tilquin opted to source organic plums in France. The Quetsche d'Alsace was sweet and dark in colour, often used for making pies and jams. The French supplier had a destoner, so Tilquin could have freshly harvested, organic, ripe, destoned plums directly delivered to his blendery.

Tilquin was as precise with his fruit blending as he was when blending his Gueuze. On top of 1,000 litres of Lambic – 400l from Boon, 400l from Lindemans, and 200l from Girardin – he added 1,000kg of plums, fermenting for four months to dry out the beer and produce a highly concentrated fruit Lambic.

From there, he and a team of four colleagues did tests of various dilutions, settling on an average dilution of 240 grams per litre. "We always taste from the lowest concentration to the highest," says Tilquin. "And we stop tasting when it's just satisfying; when you have enough fruit and still taste the Lambic."

The resultant beer – Oude Quetsche Tilquin à l'Ancienne – released in May 2012, was a hazy orange colour with aromas of plum brandy and herbal tea. The flavour was sour with a stone fruit jamminess, finishing with a dryness from both the lack of residual sugar and from the tannic skin of the plums.

"I have always said that wild yeast can speak both languages."

— PIERRE TILQUIN,
GUEUZERIE TILQUIN

Around the same time Tilquin was preparing to release his plum Lambic, he applied to become a member of HORAL. "I encountered quite a lot of resistance," he says.

IV.
ACCEPTANCE

Some of HORAL's "purists" were not happy to accept a blender operating outside the geographical boundaries of the other producers. They were reticent about granting membership to unproven producers that might damage the perception of Lambic as a regional speciality.

But Tilquin was working according to the production methods that HORAL claimed it existed to protect: making spontaneously fermented wheat beers brewed with aged hops and matured in oak that were blended and underwent a secondary fermentation in bottle. He used real fruit in his blends and produced his beers without filtering, sweetening, or pasteurisation.

Tilquin's wort was also inoculated in the coolship vessels of his suppliers, all of whom were HORAL members located in the Pajottenland and Brussels. Moreover, Gueuzerie Tilquin was virtually on the regional dividing line. His blendery in Bierghes is situated at the edge of the Senne Valley, 200 metres from Belgium's language border. "I have always said that wild yeast can speak both languages," he says.

In 2012, Gueuzerie Tilquin was accepted as a member of HORAL. Ultimately, it was the quality of his blends that swung the vote. "The more you have good Geuze on the market, the better it is for everyone," says Tilquin. Gueuzerie Tilquin has been an official stop on the Toer de Geuze since 2013. "It's a very important event," says Tilquin. "In some years, it has accounted for up to 10% of my annual sales figure."

Oude Quetsche Tilquin à l'Ancienne is still considered one of Tilquin's best blends. But he's continued to experiment and innovate with fruit that is not traditionally used in Lambic, including rhubarb, blackberries, and wine grapes.

When Tilquin joined HORAL, there were eight members. Today there are 13. Despite the growing membership, Tilquin is still the only Walloon Lambic blender in the organisation. He recently bought a brewing system and is ageing Lambic wort that he brewed at his own facility in Bierghes. He's hoping to release a 100% Tilquin blend of 1-, 2-, and 3-year old Lambics in 2025. When he does, Gueuzerie Tilquin will be the only Walloon Lambic brewery in Belgium with the only Walloon Geuze.

BIZON

A fruited Oud Bruin with a candied nose; flavours of tart cherries and ripe dates; and a soft, lingering acidic finish

| Cherry Oud Bruin
6.5% ABV | **BROUWERIJ CNUDDE**
Fabrieksstraat 8
9700 Oudenaarde | IBU: 15
EBC: 50 |

| Deep reddish-brown with an off-white head | Sour apples and red fruit, light caramel, and sweet candy | Tart cherries, red grapes, ripe dates, and a hint of vanilla, with a soft, acidic finish |

INGREDIENTS

Oudenaarde municipal water

Pilsner malt

Northern Brewer

Ester-forward ale yeast sourced from Brouwerij Roman, followed by the natural inoculation of Lactobacillus in open fermentation vats

Cherries from the brewery's trees and from Belgium's Haspengouw region

Liquid dark candi sugar

Two years' maceration in plastic vessels before blending

DISCOVER

BROUWERIJ CNUDDE
Fabrieksstraat 8
9700 Oudenaarde
(Open Saturday mornings)

NEW CASINO
Fabrieksstraat 6
9700 Oudenaarde

BIERHAL EINE CLARYSSE
(PRIK AND TIK OUDENAARDE)
Nestor de Tièrestraat 94
9700 Oudenaarde

ABOUT THE BREWERY

Founded: 1919
Brew capacity: 50hl
Annual production: 150hl

OTHER BEERS PRODUCED BY THE BREWERY

Cnudde Bruin: Oud Bruin, 4.9% ABV

RECOMMENDED FOOD PAIRING

Rabbit, potato, and carrot stew, cooked in Bizon

CEMETERY JUICE

Cnudde's Bizon beer is inextricably linked to the lives and deaths of the local community. They don't just drink it; they might even be in it.

I.
OHIO BRIDGE

In the cemetery of Saint Eligius Church in the village of Eine, thousands of gravestones mark where former residents now rest in peace.

Einenaars claim that the village's groundwater passes underneath the cemetery, and that when it rains, the water seeps through the graves and collects nutrients from the dead bodies. This water is used by the brewery located right beside the graveyard, Brouwerij Cnudde. One of the three brothers who owns the brewery, Lieven Cnudde, says that this gives their beers a "special taste." Locals refer to Cnudde beer as *kerkhofsop*, or "cemetery juice."

When pushed to confirm whether his beers contain traces of Eine's dead, Cnudde smiles: "It's a circular economy."

In life, the brewery's presence stretches to almost every village occasion: the annual Einse Fietel festival, baptisms, weddings, and funerals. In death, Einenaars give back to the village's beer, contributing the nutrients of their bones to the glasses of Cnudde which will be enjoyed for years to come by future generations.

All generations in Eine know that the brewery's logo features a bison: a broad, muscular animal with a shaggy coat. The symbol appears elsewhere in Eine. Two concrete bison statues stand on each side of the river Scheldt which runs through the village, memorialising something that happened here, at what is now known as the Ohio Bridge.

On 1 November 1918, during the First World War – only months before Brouwerij Cnudde opened – the Ohio National Guard's 37th Infantry Division crossed the Scheldt at Eine to attack the heavily fortified German Hindenburg Line.

Their operation was a crushing blow for the Germans, and 10 days later, the First World War came to an end. The depictions of bisons on the Ohio Bridge in Eine show animals of incredible power, hardwired to protect. They have come to be a symbol here, of the strength of the community.

II.
LOUIS

Lieven, Steven, and Pieter Cnudde grew up in the house beside the brewery. The building used to be a soap factory, and was converted by their great-grandfather Alphonsius Cnudde in 1919. They remember how their father Louis Cnudde produced just one beer for sale: Cnudde Bruin, a brown mixed-fermentation beer with notes of burnt caramel and red fruits, and a dry, mildly acidic finish.

But they also remember their father dabbling in small quantities of beer for his own consumption, using cherries from the garden in front of their house.

As Louis Cnudde was approaching retirement, he told his sons not to continue with the family brewery. The Cnudde brothers had already established careers for themselves. Lieven was a mathematics teacher and politician. Steven was an engineer. Pieter was a lawyer. But the brewery of their childhood was on the verge of disappearing, the same brewery that their parents and grandparents and great-grandparents had toiled to keep alive. "It was all of our youth," says Lieven Cnudde of the brewery. "It was everything."

"It was all of our youth. It was everything."

— LIEVEN CNUDDE,
BROUWERIJ CNUDDE

The three Cnudde brothers took over from their father in 1993, each working in a part-time capacity. They decided to brew just three times a year, each batch 5,000 litres, and they would sell their beer only in Eine and neighbouring Oudenaarde.

Louis Cnudde was there to advise his sons, their own children set to become the fifth generation of Cnuddes to watch their parents brew Oud Bruin in the Fabrieksstraat under the shadow of the Eine bison.

But when Louis Cnudde passed away on 22 November 1995, aged 69, the brothers were on their own. They decided to brew a new beer, one based on the cherry beer their father had so loved.

III.

PUUR KRIEK

The Cnudde brothers used the Cnudde Bruin as the base for their new cherry beer. They sourced ale yeast from Brouwerij Roman in Oudenaarde and started working with Brouwerij Strubbe in Ichtegem to bottle their beer.

Guided by tradition and family precedent, the brothers used archaic equipment and old-fashioned process to produce their beer. Their mash vessel was an old copper tun with a mechanical stirring arm. They boiled the wort in large battered copper kettles. The beer was chilled on a Baudelot cooler, in which wort, exposed to the air, runs down the side of a series of pipes filled with cold water.

They fermented their new beer in a large, open vat, and their lagering tanks were repurposed milk containers in a refrigerated room. Finally, they macerated a portion of the beer on 30 kilograms of cherries, hung muslin sacks inside plastic fermenting vessels, and added liquid brown sugar to spark a new fermentation.

The cherries initially came from the garden in front of the brewery, and as demand increased, the brothers obtained them from the orchard beside Lieven Cnudde's house one kilometre away. Today, they source cherries from the Haspengouw, the country's largest fruit-growing region. The cherries needed to be destemmed before being used, and so every Kriek harvest turned into a big party at Brouwerij Cnudde. In the courtyard, friends, family, and locals volunteered to pick the cherry stems one by one, bottles of Cnudde Bruin served as they worked.

After two years of maceration, the Cnuddes had what they described as *Puur Kriek*, but because it was so intense, pithy, and jammy, they blended it back again, in the ratio of two thirds Oud Bruin and one third *Puur Kriek*. There was no doubt about the name of the new beer: "Bizon."

IV.
"TEARS AND TEARS"

On Friday, 26 September 2014, family members of the soldiers who served in the Ohio National Guard's 37th Infantry Division walked onto the Ohio Bridge and threw roses into the Scheldt river to remember those who fought here and saved the village.

"Tears and tears," says Chris De Waele, Lieven Cnudde's friend and a retired lieutenant colonel in the Belgian Army, when describing the intensity of that moment. "It was a special day for the families and for our town. It was very emotional."

After the short ceremony, the whole party walked the 500 metres from the Ohio Bridge to Brouwerij Cnudde. Suits and military uniforms mingled in the brewery garden. A marching band played as a pair of flagpole bearers held aloft an American flag beside a Belgian one. Beers were handed out.

The Americans told Lieven Cnudde that this Bizon beer was very different to what they drank back home. It poured a deep reddish brown, with a light caramel and candy nose, and flavours hinting at tart cherries, blackcurrants, and ripe dates, eventually finishing with a soft, lingering acidic finish.

They were drinking a beer that represented the work of the Einenaars and the Cnudde family over the 100 years since the battle for Ohio Bridge; one which had been filtered through the decomposing bodies of previous generations of Einenaars who could contribute once again to this community on the banks of the Scheldt.

CUVÉE FREDDY

*An intense, dry, jammy beer with red fruit and chocolate flavours;
an oaky, tannic character; and a deep, vinous finish*

| Oud Bruin
8% ABV | **BROUWERIJ ALVINNE**
Vaartstraat 4a
8552 Moen | IBU: 5
EBC: 100 |

 Dark brown with an off-white head

 Plums, molasses, and chocolate

 Fruity and vinous, with a dry, oaky finish

INGREDIENTS

Moen municipal water

Pilsner malt, Pale Ale malt, Munich malt, wheat malt, Cara 120 malt

Nominal addition of an unspecified European hop variety

Alvinne's house yeast, Morpheus, a mixed culture of two strains of Saccharomyces cerevisiae and one strain of Lactobacillus

Dark candi sugar and glucose syrup

Six months in a French oak barrel previously used for red wine

DISCOVER

BROUWERIJ ALVINNE
Vaartstraat 4a
8552 Moen
(Open only on special occasions, but brewery visits are possible by appointment)

CAFÉ SPORTWERELD – BIJ JULO
Ter Moude 39
8552 Zwevegem

ETRE GOURMET (LA CAVE À BIÈRES)
Chaussée d'Enghien 20
1480 Tubize

RECOMMENDED FOOD PAIRING

Raspberry cheesecake

ABOUT THE BREWERY

Founded: 2004
Brew capacity: 20hl
Annual production: 800hl

OTHER BEERS PRODUCED BY THE BREWERY

Sigma: Oud Bruin, 8% ABV

Phi: Blonde Sour, 8% ABV

Cuvée Sofie: Barrel-Aged Blonde Sour, 8% ABV

Omega: Blonde Sour, 6% ABV

Wild West: Barrel-Aged Blonde Sour, 6% ABV

GOD OF DREAMS

Cuvée Freddy is produced using Brouwerij Alvinne's house yeast, Morpheus, named after the ancient Greek god of dreams. Not only has Morpheus helped Alvinne set its beers apart, but it's enabled the brewery's owners to chase their own dreams.

I.
IDENTITY

Glenn Castelein began his brewery as a home-brew project with some family members in 2002 and named it after *alvinnen* – elves and fairies he says were supposedly found in the swamps around castles in Flanders. When they received excise approval to begin brewing commercially in 2004, the name stuck, but it didn't fit. "We didn't want to be yet another fairytale brewery," says Castelein, in reference to the dragons, gnomes, devils, and trolls found across numerous Belgian beer brands.

In 2007, Castelein and his family bought a 5hl brewing system and a tiny building in the village of Heule, brewing mostly classic Belgian ales: a Blonde, a Blonde Extra, a Brown, and a Tripel. Castelein wanted the identity of the brewery to be rooted not in fairytale, but in a sense of place. Because of that, he dreamed about adding another beer style to the roster – Oud Bruin.

Heule is located in the heart of Belgium's Oud Bruin territory: the Leiestreek region that encompasses the cities of Kortrijk, Roeselare, and Oudenaarde. Oud Bruin beers are mixed-fermentation and rich in flavour, but also accessible. They pour reddish-brown and present as malty, fruity, aged, and somewhat acidic. Their malt profile can range from caramel to toast, and their acidity from soft tartness to a winey, vinegar-like character. They can be dry and tannic, or balanced out with a full-bodied sweetness.

But for all their virtues, these beers are difficult and time-consuming to produce. They're also difficult to describe, and therefore to sell. (Some beer commentators distinguish between wood-aged Flanders Red and stainless-steel-aged Oud Bruin, adding to the complexity.) There is no single defined production method; some producers blend a Blonde Ale with a brown foeder beer, others brown beers of different stock.

Castelein knew he was confronting a niche beer style with a niche market. If he were to embark on such a lengthy and commercially risky project, he'd need something special to set Alvinne apart.

II.
MORPHEUS

Meanwhile, Marc De Keukeleire was bored. He worked at a large company with 15,000 employees that produced cleaning and hygiene products, and although he loved his job, he was on the lookout for a hobby to better fuel his interest in food and drink. "There's something missing in my life," he said. In search of fulfilment, De Keukeleire started homebrewing. He dreamed of one day working in his own brewery.

In 2008, he went on holiday near Mérinchal, a town on the border of the Auvergne and Limousin regions – the least populated area in the whole of France. "Nature, woods, and cows," says De Keukeleire of the location. He had ticked off all the tourist attractions nearby and had finished reading the stack of books he'd brought. Looking for something to do, he decided to catch some native yeast.

"The commercial yeasts are very one-dimensional. There's no other mixed-fermentation strain that is as fruity as the Morpheus."

— GLENN CASTELEIN,
BROUWERIJ ALVINNE

De Keukeleire set an agar plate out in the open air for a couple of days. When he got home to Belgium, he patiently cultivated the yeast across batches and eventually isolated a strain that he felt provided the best results in his homebrews. Lab analysis at KU Leuven showed it was a mixed culture of two strains of Saccharomyces cerevisiae (a brewer's yeast type most often used in the production of ales) and one strain of Lactobacillus (a lactic acid bacteria which produces acidity). The yeast would be perfect for mixed fermentations.

De Keukeleire decided to name the yeast culture after the ancient Greek god of dreams: Morpheus. Just as Morpheus shaped the dreams of slumbering beings, De Keukeleire hoped his yeast would shape his beers – and help him realise his dream of owning a brewery. To learn more, he signed up to a homebrew class offered by a local brewer, Glenn Castelein of Brouwerij Alvinne.

III.
SIGMA

Castelein was excited to brew with Morpheus. It was alcohol-tolerant and kicked off very fruity aromas and flavours, ranging from banana and peach to apricot and plums, depending on the fermentation temperatures and type of wort. "The commercial yeasts are very one-dimensional," says Castelein. "There's no other mixed-fermentation strain that is as fruity as the Morpheus."

Morpheus was perfect for Oud Bruin. Castelein and De Keukeleire continued working together in the brewery outside the homebrew class at which they'd met. They began with a base beer they called Sigma – a Brown Ale of 8% ABV that was fermented with the Morpheus culture in stainless steel tanks. By keeping the bitterness

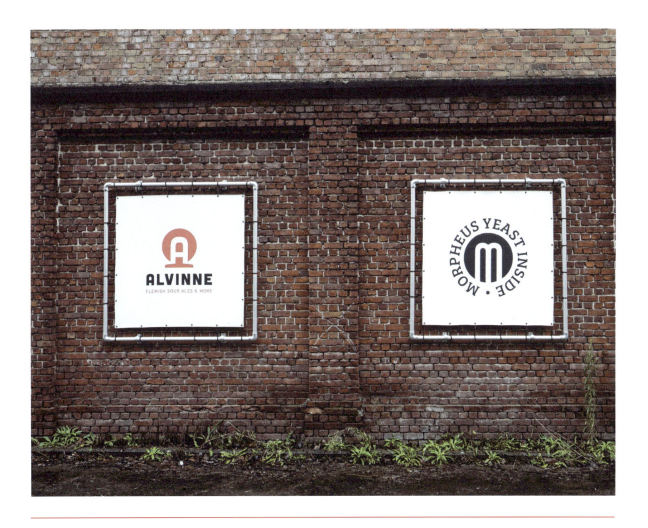

level below 12 IBU, they found they could accentuate the impact of Morpheus' Lactobacillus component. It gave them a dark, tart beer with notes of red fruits, molasses, and chocolate.

They then put Sigma in French red wine barrels for six months, the slow oxygenation helping achieve further acidification and the development of even more complex flavours. They named the resultant beer Cuvée Freddy because it was Castelein's nickname for a supportive friend who had visited the brewery around the time they were filling barrels. "Initially it was just a working name until we would finally decide what to call it when packaged," says Castelein. But the name stuck.

Cuvée Freddy, released in March 2010, was an intense, dry, and jammy beer with all the characteristics of Sigma but with an additional oaky, tannic dimension, plus enhanced fruitiness and a deep, vinous finish.

With Cuvée Freddy on the market and already in demand from importers in other countries, De Keukeleire became Castelein's business partner and the co-owner of Brouwerij Alvinne. In 2011, the brewery moved from Heule to the village of Moen, 15 kilometres deeper into the Leiestreek countryside. In its new location along the Bossuit-Kortrijk Canal, there was space for a bigger system (20hl) and more foeders and barrels. It was time for Morpheus to get to work.

IV.
FELLOWSHIP

Morpheus became Alvinne's house yeast. The brewery released other Morpheus beers named after letters in the Greek alphabet. Omega was a Blonde Sour of 6% ABV which became Wild West when barrel-aged. Phi was a Strong Blonde Sour of 8% ABV which became Cuvée Sofie when barrel-aged.

In 2019, Castelein and De Keukeleire hired a head brewer from Italy, Ricardo Murgioni, who further experimented with Morpheus, optimising fermentation and streamlining production. The yeast was stored at temperatures of -70°C in the yeast bank of KU Leuven, protected in case there were ever issues with the culture at the brewery. Alvinne started its own beer club in 2018 – "Alvinne's Fellowship Of Exceptional Ales" – and in 2021, it was awarded Brewery of the Year at the Belgian Beer Awards Digitaal Festival.

Because Castelein, De Keukeleire, and Murgioni don't feel like their beers adhere to traditional mixed-fermentation styles in the Leiestreek, they've chosen to describe them not as "Oud Bruin" or "Flemish Red" but as "Flemish Sour Ale." Today, 70% of the beers Alvinne produces are what they call Flemish Sour Ales. They have a clear identity; one linked to the owners' interpretation of this regional speciality.

"Alvinne" had been a reference to elves and fairies. But the mythology around *alvinnen* also included stories about fallen angels who would tempt men in their dreams. Today, Morpheus does all the seducing.

Hops deliver bitterness, aroma, foam stability, and preservative qualities. The second part of their Latin name, *Humulus lupulus*, means "small wolf." These are the *hidden beers* that express the howl of the hop.

WOLF PACK

HARZINGTON

A citrus-forward Hazy IPA, produced in the forests of Wallonia but inspired by the brewers of Vermont

Hazy IPA
6.5% ABV

MISERY BEER CO.
Manoir de Harzé
Pouhon 22
4920 Harzé

IBU: 65
EBC: 8

Hazy orange-blonde with a fluffy white head

Pink grapefruit, orange, and melon

Citrus flavours with a firm bitterness in the finish

INGREDIENTS

Local spring water

Pilsner malt, Pale Ale malt, malted wheat, Golden Naked Oat flakes

Amarillo, Centennial

New-England-style Vermont ale yeast

DISCOVER

MISERY BEER CO.
Manoir de Harzé
Pouhon 22
4920 Harzé

L'ANNEXE
Rue Roture 13a
4020 Liège

RECOMMENDED FOOD PAIRING

Spicy Thai beef salad
(laab neua)

ABOUT THE BREWERY

Founded: 2017 / **Opened**: 2020
Brew capacity: 10hl
Annual production: 700hl

OTHER BEERS PRODUCED BY THE BREWERY

Hopduction: DDH American Pale Ale, 6% ABV

Holy Moly: DDH American Pale Ale, 6% ABV

Concrete Jungle: DDH Double IPA, 8.5% ABV

Paradis: DDH Double IPA, 7% ABV

MISERY IN PARADISE

The owners of Misery Beer Co. have faced real hardship. But through misery, they've been inspired by their community to keep going.

I.
VERMONT

In 2018, Rémy Perée and Samia Patsalides crossed into the U.S. from Québec to visit a village 60 kilometres from Vermont's biggest city, Burlington. In Stowe, they were surrounded by beautiful forests and mountain terrain. But they weren't there for the nature. They'd come for The Alchemist.

Before Canada, the Belgian couple had lived in Louvain-La-Neuve. Perée was from a family of brewing engineers; Patsalides' family had worked as academics. Together, they dreamt of escaping the misery of city life. "We were looking for a new start," says Patsalides. That new start began with a brewing course at L'Institut Brassicole du Québec in Montreal. While there, they made the trip to Vermont to visit a brewery that had pioneered a new way of producing hoppy styles.

The Alchemist used fruitier, less attenuative yeasts in its IPAs, delivering more yeast-driven aromas and flavours than both the English-style IPAs previously favoured on the East Coast and bracingly bitter West Coast IPAs. In addition, it promoted the greater use of dry-hopping, resulting in hazy, refreshing beer with bright minerality and extravagant hop character.

Before The Alchemist's owners, John and Jen Kimmich, had opened their brewery in Stowe, they ran a brewpub and then a small production brewery in Waterbury, Vermont. Hurricane Irene in August 2011 put their brewpub under several feet of water, and subsequently out of business. But the Kimmichs rebuilt, never compromising on how they wanted to brew or on their community-focused sustainability initiatives.

Inspired by the resilience of the Kimmichs and the innovation of Vermont's beer scene, Rémy Perée and Samia Patsalides returned to Belgium to continue their dream – to open their own brewery.

II.
THE HOUSE FROM THE NOVEL

The Manoir de Harzé is a beautiful old Ardennes manor house that reminded Perée and Patsalides of Stephen King's novel "Misery." In King's horror story, a writer is injured following a drunken car accident during a snowstorm and is dragged to a remote country house by a deranged nurse who proceeds to torture him. "It was like a haunted house," says Patsalides of the manor. "When we visited it the first time, it was very old and creepy."

The manor had been used as a 17th-century hotel, a lab for water-dowsing scientists, and a Second World War communication centre. By the time Perée and Patsalides came across it, it had fallen into ruin.

"I always say it's the novel," says Perée of the reason they named their brewery Misery Beer Co. "But the community in Liège and here in the village, they know. It's because we are all living in the same misery."

The Liège valley experienced abrupt economic decline in the late 20th century, after its mines and steel industry were closed. Perée saw it firsthand, when Anheuser-Busch-InBev bought the Piedboeuf family brewery

> "The day it happened, I understood much more about the community and why I have to build something for the village."
>
> — RÉMY PERÉE,
> MISERY BEER CO.

in Jupille-sur-Meuse and devastated its workforce, including his father, uncle, and grandfather. "In Liège, the people have to fight every day," he says.

After buying the manor with their life savings in 2018, Perée and Patsalides spent almost a year and half renovating. They worked hard on their beers too, producing a 6.5% ABV Vermont-inspired IPA – a hazy, fruity beer with pronounced hop aromatics and an enticing bitterness. They called it Harzington, a portmanteau of Harzé, where their manor is located, and Burlington, the place that inspired the brewery.

But then, on 14 July 2021, torrential rain began pouring down in the Liège valley, a turn of events that would mirror the fate of the Kimmichs' first brewery in Vermont. It was the start of one of the most catastrophic floods Belgium would ever experience.

III.
TRIAGE

Record rains fell for 48 hours in Liège. Entire towns were washed away. Tens of thousands of people were evacuated; 26,000 houses were destroyed. Forty-three people were killed. Six days after the rains, Belgium declared a national day of mourning.

Rémy Perée and Samia Patsalides had managed to secure a pump. They tried pumping water out from the floor of the manor, but the stock of beers in the cellar was submerged under nearly three metres of water, and some brewing equipment had been destroyed.

A local fireman arrived. He was not there to help, but for triage. He told them to evacuate immediately and took their pump for use elsewhere, leaving by the

forested hills to avoid the flooded roads. "It's like a doctor who's going to try and help someone he can save," says Patsalides of the fireman. "Here, he can't save it."

Perée and Patsalides, their visiting friends, and the six children in the house were left to face rising water and the oncoming darkness of the night without gas, electricity, or food.

But all of a sudden, local people who had already lost their houses started arriving at the manor. They came with dry clothes, food, and sandbags. And another pump.

"All day, I was crying," says Perée. "It was really emotional for us. They lost everything and they came here just to help me. It's that day I realised I have to take care of my community. We are not alone."

"It saved the brewery," says Patsalides.

> "It's because we are all living in the same misery."
>
> — RÉMY PERÉE,
> MISERY BEER CO.

IV.
LOOKING UP

By the following day, with their sandbags and their pump and their shovels, Misery and the locals of Harzé had quelled the damage of the floods.

Even though the clean-up would take several more weeks, Perée and Patsalides opened the taproom amidst the carnage – mud everywhere, fallen trees, broken buildings, and exhausted volunteers whose boots were soaked with dirty floodwater.

"The day it happened, I understood much more about the community and why I have to build something for the village," says Perée.

When the roads were clear enough to drive, Perée and Patsalides loaded their van with whatever beer was salvageable and drove to a Red Cross drop-off point in Liège. Misery's Harzington provided volunteers with an opportunity to sit with their colleagues and pretend things were normal, even for just half an hour.

Two small rivers converge at the entrance to Misery Beer Co., each named after the townlands through which they flow: Pouhon and Paradis. It was at this confluence that the floods became most serious. Shortly after the floods, Perée and Patsalides released a Double IPA called Paradis to commemorate the experience.

Rémy Perée and Samia Patsalides look up at the townland of Paradis every day. From their manor, its majestic forested banks seem almost beyond reach. Perée and Patsalides will always be down here, nestled low in Pouhon at the foot of the hills, where life seems harder. But they never complain and they've no regrets. "Life is harder now," says Patsalides. "But it's more beautiful."

In Harzé, you must walk past the brewery in Pouhon to get to the neighbouring townland of Paradis. You have to traverse the dirt to enjoy the picturesque views from the forested hillsides. You have to pass through Misery to get to Paradise.

KEIKOPPENBIER

*A grassy, herbal, and subtly spicy organic Belgian Blonde Ale,
now produced by a farm brewery in West Flanders*

	TERREST BREWERY	
Belgian Blonde Ale 6.1% ABV	Vlastraat 1 8650 Houthulst	IBU: 30 EBC: 12

Deep gold with a pillowy white head	Grassy, floral, and mildly spicy, with notes of biscuit, honey, and a touch of zesty grapefruit	Medium-bodied, herbal, and citrusy, with a satisfying bitter finish

INGREDIENTS

Houthulst municipal water

Pilsner malt, Munich malt

Pilgrim, Goldings, Cascade

Belgian ale yeast

RECOMMENDED FOOD PAIRING

Grilled halibut fillet
with pesto alla genovese

ABOUT THE BREWERY

Founded: 2021
Brew capacity: 18hl
Annual production: 300hl

DISCOVER

TERREST BREWERY
Vlastraat 1
8650 Houthulst

GOESTE RESTAURANT
Grote Markt 28
8970 Poperinge

DRANKEN TOMMELIN
Dikkebusseweg 308
8908 Ieper

ABOUT DE PLUKKER FARM

Founded: 1954
Location: Elverdingseweg 14A,
8970 Poperinge
Hectares: 12.5 (hops)
Hop varieties: Golding, Pilgrim,
WGV, Fuggle, Phoenix, Challenger,
Cascade, Centennial (100% organic)

ABOUT TERREST FARM

Founded: 1988
Location: Vlastraat 1,
8650 Houthulst
Hectares: 50 (hops, barley, cattle)
Hop varieties: Magnum, Goldings
Grain cultivation: Barley
(3–5 hectares)

OTHER BEERS PRODUCED BY THE BREWERY

Terrest Golden Tripel:
Tripel, 8% ABV

Rookop: Belgian Brown Ale,
6.5% ABV

Tripel Plukker: Tripel,
7.5% ABV

All Inclusive: Belgian Strong
Blonde Ale, 8% ABV

DAY OF REST

The story of Keikoppenbier reminds us that on any journey, there's a time to seize the day – but there's also a time to rest.

I.
THE PICKER

"Cobblestone-head." That's the nickname given to the inhabitants of Poperinge by their neighbouring towns. *Keikop* refers to the stubborn, hard-headed nature of Poperingers – a name used as far back as the 14th century.

The nickname was the inspiration for Brouwerij De Plukker's first and flagship beer: Keikoppenbier – "the beer of the cobblestone-headed" – created by hop farmer Joris Cambie and brewer Kris Langouche in 2011. *Pluk* in Flemish refers to "plucking" or "picking"; the Latin expression *carpe diem* ("seize the day") translates into *pluk de dag*. Their brewery name, therefore, refers to "the picker" who plucks the day as it's ripe.

Poperinge is known for hops. The city is home to the National Hop Museum and hosts a triannual Beer and Hop Festival. Poperinge's farmers grow three-quarters of all hops cultivated in Belgium. Cambie had been running his family's organic hop farm in Poperinge since his father retired in 1993, and had built a strong reputation for quality.

In the summer of 2023, Valerie Van der Bauwhede started interning on Cambie's hop farm as part of "an introduction to agriculture" class. She was no stranger to the business: Her parents ran both a cattle farm and a tobacco factory and, in 2021, Van der Bauwhede co-founded her own brewery with her father, Johan Van der Bauwhede – Terrest Brewery.

During her internship at De Plukker farm, Van der Bauwhede learned how hardy you need to be to grow hops. "You've got farmers and then you've got hop growers," says Cambie. "The other farmers say that you have to be crazy to grow hops." But Van der Bauwhede was excited to learn from Cambie. She wanted to *pluk de dag*. "I thought this could be a good place to start."

II.
HARD-HEADED

Keikoppenbier is a hoppy Belgian Blonde Ale of 6.1% ABV. Brewed with organic Pilsner and Munich malts for a deep-golden hue and biscuity profile, it's fermented with a Belgian ale yeast strain for subtle notes of orange and apricot. The hops come from Cambie's farm: Pilgrim as a bittering addition, and Goldings and Cascade for a grassy, floral, and spicy character.

In recent years, Keikoppenbier had become a mainstay in bars, cafés, and bottle shops in the region, a classic and easy-drinking Blonde that spoke to Poperinge's identity. De Plukker even opened its own café in the city centre, managed by Langouche and his wife Shirley D'hooghe, the Plukker Pub. Cambie and Langouche had big plans to open a larger production facility, but also to bring their existing brewing system to a new visitor-focused location the city would call the "Centre of Hop and Beer," just beside the National Hop Museum.

Meanwhile, Van der Bauwhede was building her brewery in Terrest, a hamlet in Houthulst. Ask locals how the hamlet got its name and you'll hear several legends. One is that it comes from the Flemish *Ter Herst* – "The Ridge" – because it sits on the Westrozebeke Ridge. Another is that it was named by Julius Caesar as he passed through the area, searching for raised land on which to set up camp. Seeing the Terrest hill, Caesar is said to have exclaimed: "Terra est!" ("There is land!")

KEIKOPPENBIER

> "You've got farmers and then you've got hop growers. The other farmers say that you have to be crazy to grow hops."
>
> — JORIS CAMBIE,
> DE PLUKKER FARM

Where they could, the Van der Bauwhedes worked with their own Magnum and Goldings hops and barley. While Van der Bauwhede was interning at De Plukker farm, she watched Cambie and Langouche work at De Plukker brewery. She was not a *keikop*, but maybe one day she could be as "cobblestone-headed" as the Poperingers. Maybe one day Terrest could have its own Keikoppenbier.

III.
OVER THE RIDGE

By 2022, De Plukker had been running successfully for more than a decade, but its owners were making little profit and licensing restrictions meant expansion wasn't possible. Langouche was getting tired of the manual labour, climbing into the tanks to scrub them after each use.

Then, the plan for the larger production facility fell through at the last minute. The "Centre of Hop and Beer" would now take several years to realise. De Plukker could not continue in its current form.

Langouche and D'hooghe closed the Plukker Pub in December 2022. Cambie tried to keep a slimmed-down brewery operational, but he needed to prioritise his hop farm. He was a 58-year-old widower with five children, none of whom were interested in taking over the brewery. "For 11 years, we made good beer," he says. "But we didn't make much money. We don't need to prove anything anymore."

Valerie Van der Bauwhede learned from Cambie about the situation at De Plukker. She had since produced Terrest's first and only beer – Terrest Golden Tripel – and in August 2023, it was awarded a gold medal in the "Belgian-style Tripel" category at the 2023 World Beer Awards. Van der Bauwhede pitched the idea of taking over the De Plukker brands to her father. "It was not a big discussion," she says. "He said, 'Let's do it.'" *Pluk de dag.*

In the Van der Bauwhede family, Cambie and Langouche saw fellow farmers from West Flanders, and they agreed to talk. "For them, it was very important to find a partner who has the same values as they did," says Van der Bauwhede. One pair was looking down a ridge; the other ascending it.

> "For them, it was very important to find a partner who has the same values as they did."
>
> — VALERIE VAN DER BAUWHEDE,
> TERREST BREWERY

IV.
TE RUSTE

As of 24 September 2023, Terrest now runs two product lines: Terrest and De Plukker. The Van der Bauwhedes have continued brewing Keikoppenbier, and say they'll remain faithful to the recipes and processes that Cambie and Langouche developed. They will also continue using Cambie's organic hops in the De Plukker beers, and their own grain and hops in the Terrest range.

Van der Bauwhede acknowledges the enormity of the task of taking over a beloved Poperinge brand. "[Keikoppenbier] was the child of Joris and Kris," she says. "It's a lot of pressure to produce the same quality." Langouche helped the Van der Bauwhedes with their very first brew. "It's a nice brewery with driven owners," says Langouche of Terrest. "I think they will do a good job with the De Plukker beers. I'm glad that the beers can still exist."

When you ask Van der Bauwhede how Terrest got its name, she mentions the famous legends about the ridge and Julius Caesar, but she proffers another story: that the name of the hamlet comes from the Flemish, *te ruste*, meaning "to rest." "If they drove up the hill here with horse-and-carts, then the horse needed to rest. That makes a bit more sense for me."

Terrest's acquisition of De Plukker's brands was announced in February 2024. For Cambie, it was a bittersweet moment: the end of a brewing adventure, no more days to be plucked at the brewery. But it was a fond farewell, with the knowledge that the stubborn Keikoppenbier would survive. *Imperium mortuum est; vivat imperium.* Sometimes, no matter how hardheaded you are, it's time to rest so you're ready for life's next ridge.

ELDORADO

A citrus-forward and resinous beer, which combines the juiciness of an IPA and the fruitiness of an iconic Belgian yeast strain

Belgian IPA 7.5% ABV	**BRASSERIE DES CHAMPS** Rue de la Tour 15 5190 Spy (Jemeppe-sur-Sambre)	IBU: 55 EBC: 14
 Deep gold with a bright white head of foam	 Tangerine, grapefruit, blueberry, and lime	 Fruity and slightly resinous, with a dry, bitter finish

INGREDIENTS

Jemeppe-sur-Sambre municipal water, adjusted for pH

Pilsner malt, wheat malt, Cara Ruby malt, Cara 120 malt

El Dorado, Citra, Simcoe, Mosaic, Motueka

Orval ale yeast, American ale yeast

RECOMMENDED FOOD PAIRING

Hard, raw-milk cow's cheese, such as Emmont of
FERME DE LA GROSSE HAIE
Rue de Fosses 222
5060 Sambreville

DISCOVER

BRASSERIE DES CHAMPS
Rue de la Tour 15
5190 Spy (Jemeppe-sur-Sambre)
(The brewery taproom is open only during events)

BARNABEER
Rue de Bruxelles 39
5000 Namur

BEER, WINE AND SPIRIT
Rue de l'Artisanat 14
5020 Namur

ABOUT THE BREWERY

Founded: 2017 (with a rebranding in 2022 of Eldorado from Brasserie de la Sambre to Brasserie de la Tour, and another rebranding in 2024 to Brasserie des Champs)
Brew capacity: 8hl
Annual production: 200hl

OTHER BEERS PRODUCED BY THE BREWERY

BRASSERIE DES CHAMPS
Spyls: Pilsner, 6.5% ABV

BRASSERIE DES CHAMPS
Cuvée de Spy: Belgian Strong Blonde Ale, 9.6% ABV

BRASSERIE DE LA SAMBRE
Åbricot: Fruited Saison, 7.1% ABV

BRASSERIE DE LA SAMBRE
Soyouz: Russian Imperial Stout, 13.7% ABV

MINING FOR GOLD

El Dorado – the legendary lost "City of Gold" – is often seen as a metaphor for humanity's quest for the unattainable. Through his beer, Jean-Christophe Larsimont embarked on his own search for purpose.

I.
JACKHAMMER

On 21 December 2021, Jean-Christophe Larsimont picked up his pneumatic jackhammer and began drilling a hole in the wall of the 13th-century farmhouse that would house his family's new brewery.

Ferme de la Tour in the municipality of Jemeppe-sur-Sambre was once a *ferme château*, a farmhouse fortified for defence. The stone walls were 40cm thick. Some parts that broke off weighed as much as 60kg.

Formerly a biomedical academic and researcher of skin cancer, but today working in the manufacture of brewing equipment, Larsimont was drilling to create an opening that would connect the mezzanine of the production space with the soon-to-be taproom.

Larsimont worked for five full days, blinded by his own sweat as he rammed the heavy jackhammer up against the wall, taking breaks every few minutes because his muscles were aching. A neighbour messaged Larsimont to remind him that it was now Christmas Day, and that maybe he should go back to his family.

Jean-Christophe Larsimont's brewery produces beers under two brand names. The De la Sambre brand has become a darling of the beer enthusiast community, offering a range of wild Saisons, fruit experiments, and Russian Imperial Stouts. The Des Champs brand,

"Miners have this strong relationship with work and working hard. We never stop."

— JEAN-CHRISTOPHE LARSIMONT,
BRASSERIE DES CHAMPS

on the other hand, is intended for the people of the village, its beers more accessible: a Pilsner, a Belgian Blonde, a Belgian Golden Strong Ale, and most importantly, a Belgian IPA called Eldorado.

El Dorado is best known as a legendary lost city in South America – the "City of Gold." The illusory destination of numerous failed expeditions, El Dorado is today used as a metaphor for an elusive ultimate prize; something sought-after that may never be found. Jean-Christophe Larsimont, jackhammer in hand, was on an expedition of his own: to find purpose in hard work.

II.
HARD WORK

Larsimont's brewery is located in Spy, a small village surrounded by three of the four major coal mines in Wallonia, all of which are now shuttered.

His father, Yves Larsimont, had worked in the mines here, as did Yves' father and grandfather before him. The region relied on the coal industry for employment, but 20th-century deindustrialization ushered in a period of economic deprivation. When Roton colliery in Farciennes closed its doors in 1984, the last mine in Wallonia to do so, the Larsimonts had to find other work.

Yves Larsimont was sent off to the army. On his return, he fell into manual labour, working hard to provide for his family. The transition was a difficult one.

In 2010, when 21-year-old Jean-Christophe Larsimont was finishing his degree at the University of Namur, his father died by suicide.

His family dealt with the tragedy by pulling closer together: His mother Dominique Rolland, his brother Thibaut Larsimont, his aunt Marie-Aline Rolland, his partner Maëlle Winant, and her father Serge Majerus.

They would find their way forward through hard work. "Miners have this strong relationship with work and

working hard," says Larsimont. "We never stop."

Brewing was physical work that produced a tangible result, one that could be shared with the people around you. The family started homebrewing, honing recipes in 2013 and 2014. In 2015, they took a recipe for a Belgian IPA to nearby brewery Brasserie Saint-Lazare in Mons, where owner Jean-Philippe Mottoul allowed them to brew themselves. Next, they began the years-long, back-breaking renovation of the farm. In 2017, they officially released their first beer: Eldorado.

III.
BACKBONE

At the time of Eldorado's commercial release, there were few beers in Belgium that combined the juiciness of an IPA and the fruitiness of a Belgian yeast strain.

Larsimont was able to source the yeast he uses for Eldorado "through a friend" at the world-renowned Orval Trappist Abbey, located within driving distance of Jemeppe-sur-Sambre. Orval's top-fermenting yeast – clean, highly attenuating, and fruit-forward – is known for its cornucopia of esters: red grape, plum, apple, and orange peel. Keen to avoid the peppery, spicy phenols of some other Belgian yeasts, and determined that Eldorado would ferment dry, Larsimont also pitched an American ale yeast to finish fermentation.

To this golden, fruity, and dry ale, he added a bounty of hops. The centrepiece was El Dorado, used both as a bittering and aroma hop, and derived from a Humulus neomexicanus subspecies that has been growing wild in the dry mountain regions of New Mexico for the last million years. "You cannot use it alone," says Larsimont of the hop known for its pear, candy, and watermelon character. "It has a profile that makes the beer overcloying very quickly. But it creates the backbone of flavour."

On top of this backbone, he mined the grapefruit character of Citra hops, the pine and citrus zest of Simcoe, the blueberry and papaya flavours of Mosaic, and the lime notes of Motueka.

> "We are not qualified to discuss what a kilo of cherries is worth. You do not know the sweat and tears and blood that went into it."
>
> — JEAN-CHRISTOPHE LARSIMONT,
> BRASSERIE DES CHAMPS

Importantly, Larsimont used a small proportion of Cara Ruby malt – alongside Pilsner malt and wheat malt – for a delicacy of texture, improved head retention, and a golden colour to match the name of the beer.

IV.
EXPEDITION

Larsimont's biomedical studies centred on skin cancer, but he moved away from academia because he would have had to travel for a research position, and didn't want to be far from the family he loved.

He admits there's no comparison in the level of meaning between his previous job as a cancer researcher and his current one as a brewer. "I cannot match it," he says. "You cannot do better than trying to make people better, improving their health, helping them survive longer, helping them stay with their family."

But just as his family before him served their communities by mining, he now serves his by brewing. It's likely to take a whole lifetime to find the purpose he seeks: an El Dorado expedition of his own.

Hard work is at the centre of the Larsimonts' operations, and through their two very different brands of De la Sambre and Des Champs, the family caters to all tastes. The beers also evince a respect for the hard work of others. Larsimont never questions the price asked by his suppliers for the grain, hops, or fruit he uses, even if it means that his beers are more expensive. "We are not qualified to discuss what a kilo of cherries is worth," says Larsimont. "You do not know the sweat and tears and blood that went into it."

In the taproom space now cleared by Larsimont's jackhammering, there hangs above the bar a large bronze logo of one of his brands. The same symbol appears on the glassware, coasters, and labels: a miner's lamp and two pickaxes; one to show the way, the other to help them work through the stone.

VALEIR EXTRA

A classic Belgian Blonde Ale-meets-citrusy IPA, produced by a former landscape architect who fought bravely to preserve the tradition of his wife's family – and to create a brewing legacy of his own

Belgian IPA 6.5% ABV	**BROUWERIJ CONTRERAS** Molenstraat 110 9890 Gavere	IBU: 35 EBC: 15
 Pale amber with light haze and a fluffy white head	 Stone fruits and mango, with subtle hints of pepper	 Citrusy, grassy, and grainy, with a balanced finish and a keen carbonic bite

INGREDIENTS

Local groundwater, adjusted for pH

Pilsner malt, Munich malt

Magnum, Amarillo

A proprietary fruity yeast propagated in collaboration with Ghent University

RECOMMENDED FOOD PAIRING

Baked mackerel with Cajun spice, served with a chilli, mango, and lime salsa

DISCOVER

BROUWERIJ CONTRERAS
Molenstraat 110
9890 Gavere

CAFÉ DE ROOIGEM
Baaigemstraat 183
9890 Gavere

PEDE DRINKS
SINT-LIEVENS-HOUTEM
Doelstraat 12
9520 Sint-Lievens-Houtem

ABOUT THE BREWERY

Founded: 1818
Brew capacity: 70hl
Annual production: 3,000hl

OTHER BEERS PRODUCED BY THE BREWERY

Contrapils: Pilsner, 5% ABV

Tonneke Speciale Belge: Spéciale Belge, 5% ABV

Especial Mars: Bière de Mars, 6.5% ABV

Valeir Blond: Blonde Ale, 6.5% ABV

1818: Saison, 6% ABV

TRUE VALOUR

Valeir Extra from Brouwerij Contreras represents courage in Belgian brewing – and its stoic brewer is perhaps more quintessentially Belgian than any other.

I.
RELIC

In 2005, 71-year-old brewer Willy Contreras suffered a heart attack. He was the owner and brewer of Brouwerij Contreras, an ageing facility in Gavere which he had inherited from his father, grandfather, and great-grandfather before him. He had worked there for 48 years, but now, given his bad health, the brewery's future was in doubt.

Willy Contreras hadn't been big on change, and had invested little in brewery equipment. He had continued to use open fermentation tanks and a Baudelot cooler, and didn't even label his beers until laws required him to do so beginning in the early 1990s. Up until then, consumers just had to know his colour cap code.

Now, unable to continue running the business, Willy Contreras transferred ownership of Brouwerij Contreras to his daughter, Ann. But Ann Contreras wasn't interested in running a brewery, and she left its management to her husband, Frederik De Vrieze – a practising landscape architect, not a brewer.

Willy Contreras didn't know it, but De Vrieze had been taking brewing classes in Ghent, waiting for the day when his father-in-law might pass the reins. De Vrieze would show himself to be the quintessential Belgian brewer: innovative but pragmatic, obsessed with quality and balance, and warrior-like in his quest to save the village's dying brewery.

II.
MONUMENTS

So as to preserve the legacy of his father-in-law when he took over in 2005, Frederik De Vrieze maintained production of the traditional Contreras beers he had inherited: a Spéciale Belge called Tonneke; a Bière de Mars called Especial Mars; and the house lager, Contrapils.

He also released a new beer that showed great commercial promise. His Belgian Blonde Ale of 6.5% ABV – Valeir Blond – showed off a fruity yeast character, and was dry-hopped with Sterling, an aroma hop that combined the best of its parent varieties: the spicy notes of Saaz and the bright citrus of Cascade. It would go on to spark a whole new range of Valeir beers.

Valeir was the name given to a statue in the centre of Gavere to commemorate the Battle of Gavere, which took place 500 years ago. The statue itself had been nameless, but its sullen expression resembled the face of one of Gavere's well-known inhabitants in the 1950s: a local carpenter called Valeir Stevens.

Since then, the name Valeir has become synonymous with the village. There's a Brotherhood of the Aunts and Uncles of Valeir – De Confrérie van de Tantes en Nonkels van Valeir – who wear ceremonial gowns and organise activities to promote the village. There's a Valeirkoekje, a traditional Valeir biscuit produced by a local baker. There's a restaurant located in the town's centre called 't Valeirke. The farm brewery where Brouwerij Contreras was located was even originally set up by a Valère Latte in 1818.

> "We were one of the first Belgian breweries starting with that kind of beer."
>
> — FREDERIK DE VRIEZE,
> BROUWERIJ CONTRERAS

De Vrieze's attitude matched the stoicism of the Valeir statue. He reacted not to the challenging events he faced in the brewery, but to his judgments about those events, focusing only on the things within his control. The name Valeir made it clear that this was a beer of the village. And his resurrection of the brewery went so well in those first two years that the community of Gavere would soon approach De Vrieze about a special project.

III.

DE RONDE

In 2007, Gavere was selected as the Dorp van de Ronde: Village of the Tour. The Tour was the Ronde Van Vlaanderen, the Tour of Flanders, an iconic and gruelling 265km cycling race across narrow cobblestoned hills in the Flemish Ardennes. Gavere needed a special beer to celebrate the honour, and it needed it immediately.

With very little time, De Vrieze had to think fast. He decided to base the beer on Valeir Blond, bittering with Magnum hops and dry-hopping with a new variety he had come across called Amarillo, sourced from the Yakima Valley in Washington State. It's now one of the most-used hops in the U.S., but it was almost completely unknown in Belgium in 2007.

Amarillo is known for its orange citrus character, sometimes edging into grapefruit, melon, and peach. It complemented the fruity yeast of the Valeir range perfectly. De Vrieze released the beer to the general market in 2008 as Valeir Extra.

The Contreras offering was diversifying and sales were on the rise, but working with archaic machinery was taking its toll on De Vrieze. When officers of Belgium's Federal Agency for the Safety of the Food Chain visited Contreras in 2009, they were so concerned with the state of the building and equipment that they gave De Vrieze an ultimatum: If he didn't deal with their concerns, they would be forced to close Contreras forever.

IV.

BICENTENNIAL

In 2010, De Vrieze decided to close the brewery for a full year to make investments in the milling system, fermentation vessels, and bottling equipment. "I broke everything down and started renewing bit by bit," he says. "We had to start from zero."

During that year of closure, the specifications for the brewery were completely upscaled. De Vrieze maintained the old 70hl tiled mash tun and boiling kettle, but brought in high-standard stainless steel fermentation tanks, all temperature controlled, as well as a large centrifuge for clarifying the beer and a plate filter for his Pilsner.

When he reopened, De Vrieze received approval from the Federal Agency for the Safety of the Food Chain that he could continue brewing. Because of the greater control afforded by the new equipment, Contreras' legacy brands, such as Tonneke, Especial Mars, and Contrapils, as well as the new Valeir range, were all produced to an even higher quality standard than before.

In August 2018, De Vrieze hosted an open brew day, attracting a large crowd to celebrate the 200th birthday of Brouwerij Contreras. Those in attendance enjoyed his newest beer, a Saison known simply as 1818 after the year the brewery was founded. De Confrérie van de Tantes en Nonkels van Valeir celebrated the occasion with locals. Willy Contreras was there, and when he passed away two years later, on 26 October 2020, aged 86, he did so knowing that the family brewery was thriving.

The exact meaning of the name Valeir is not certain, but it likely shares its origins with the Latin word *valor*, meaning "strong" or "morally worthy." It suggests great courage or personal bravery in battle, and denotes a particular strength of spirit that enables a person to encounter danger with fortitude.

In his fight to keep Brouwerij Contreras alive, Frederik De Vrieze has shown valour. Through his stoicism and bravery, he has proven you can modernise and innovate while remaining true to a rich brewing heritage.

During fermentation, yeast cells eat grain sugars and convert them into alcohol and carbonation. But they also create pronounced aroma and flavour compounds, which range from fruity to funky. These are the *hidden beers* showcasing the wonders of Belgian yeast.

FUNGUS KINGDOM

BIÈRE DE TABLE

*A delicate, acidic beer with a thirst-quenching dryness
and a pleasant lemony profile*

Table Beer
3.8% ABV

BRASSERIE LA JUNGLE
Studio CityGate
Rue de la Petite Île 1A
1070 Anderlecht

IBU: 25
EBC: 4

Pale gold
with a fluffy white head

Crackers, citrus,
and pears

Lemon and tangerine, with a hint
of black pepper in the finish

INGREDIENTS

Brussels municipal water
with pH adjustments

Pilsner malt, malted wheat,
flaked wheat, flaked oats

Styrian Goldings,
East Kent Goldings

French Saison yeast and
a mixed house culture of wild
yeast and bacteria

Two-month wild fermentation
in plastic cubitainers

DISCOVER

BREWDOG
Putterie 20
1000 Brussels

MALT ATTACKS
Avenue Jean Volders 18
1060 Saint-Gilles

RECOMMENDED FOOD PAIRING

Roast chicken with coriander,
thyme, oregano, and cumin,
served with a panzanella salad

ABOUT THE BLENDERY

Founded: 2020
Brew capacity: 4hl
Annual production: 175hl

OTHER BEERS PRODUCED BY THE BREWERY

Saison La Jungle:
Saison, 5.6% ABV

Bruxelles Sun: Saison, 6.9% ABV

Saison Sauvage – Prune Rouge:
Fruit Saison, 5.5% ABV

Saison Sauvage – Pêche Blanche:
Fruit Saison, 5.5% ABV

Saison Sauvage – Orange Sanguine: Fruit Saison, 5.5% ABV

DELIVERANCE

Three young Brussels brewers set out to discover their wild sides, inspired by Belgium's pastoral brewing tradition. But it wasn't the relaxing nature trip they were expecting. In Belgian beer, it's survival of the fittest: You live by the law of the jungle.

I.
WELCOME TO THE JUNGLE

While studying at university in the 2000s, Christophe Bravin, Félix Damien, and Martin Pirenne would meet up to drink beer and watch cult American movies like Michael Mann's *Heat*, Quentin Tarantino's *Pulp Fiction*, and John Boorman's 1972 thriller *Deliverance*.

In *Deliverance*, four businessmen decide to canoe down a river in the remote northern Georgia wilderness before it is dammed. The film attained cult status for its memorable poster, showing a hand grasping a shotgun pointed at the canoe, as well as one of the most famous scenes in cinema history: the "Dueling Banjos" duet. Much as the countryside seems quaint at first, it soon becomes a wilderness of terror.

Bravin compares the story of *Deliverance* to the journey of Brasserie La Jungle, the small Brussels brewery he and his friends opened in 2020.

The brewery is located at Studio CityGate, a complex of old textile warehouses in Brussels' Anderlecht region, today given over to creatives and entrepreneurs as part of an urban renewal project. Surrounded by Moroccan bakeries, Romanian cafés, and traffic jams, the brewery was named for the chaotic urban jungle that encircles it. It's a chaos Bravin, Damien, and Pirenne loved, but from which they also aspired to break free. "We were living in the city and we wanted to take a wild nature break," says Bravin. They hoped to bring pastoral beers – especially Belgian Saison – to their urban home, as a form of self-rescue; a deliverance of their own.

Bravin and his partners have spent the last four years navigating their own canoe in the choppy waters of the pandemic-era Belgian beer market. According to Bravin: "When you go down the river in the canoe, things are not always as pleasant as you first thought."

II.
SETTING THE TABLE

The trio had bonded over the beers they drank at university: Saison Dupont and Avec Les Bons Vœux from Brasserie Dupont; XX Bitter from Brasserie De Ranke; and Zinnebir from Brasserie de la Senne. Although pulled in different directions – Bravin to video editing, Damien to microbiological research, and Pirenne to television production – they were able to embark on holiday and temporary work adventures together in Canada. There, they were influenced by what they drank in Montreal beer bar Vices & Versa and at the Québec-based Brasserie Dunham (which specialised in Table Beers and Saisons).

The first beer La Jungle's founders brewed at Studio CityGate was their Bière de Table. This was not like the Table Beers of their parents' and grandparents' youth – sweet, brown ales served to children at dinner and now more likely to be found on the geriatric wards of regional hospitals or poured into Flemish stews. Instead, La Jungle's Bière de Table is a 3.8% ABV mixed-fermentation beer that better resembles a mixed-culture mini-Saison.

"When you go down the river in the canoe, things are not always as pleasant as you first thought."

— CHRISTOPHE BRAVIN,
BRASSERIE LA JUNGLE

After primary fermentation with a lab-grown French Saison yeast, they pitch their "magic blend of wild yeast and bacteria," a house culture La Jungle's founders have maintained since their homebrew days (it began as the dregs of bottles of their favourite beers from Cantillon, De Ranke, and Dutch producer Nevel Wild Ales). The beer ferments wild for two months in plastic cubitainers until the acidity rises and the sugar content drops. They then bottle-condition it for three months so that, according to Damien, "the beer is given time to fully express its wild side."

The result is a delicate and slightly acidic beer with a thirst-quenching dryness and a pleasant lemony, lactic-acid profile. The beer comes dressed in a label by artist Marie Theurier; her designs feature fruits and dense forests delivered in highly textured and colourful illustrations. Bière de Table was La Jungle's deliverance from city beer, but the waters were about to get choppy.

III.
CHOPPY WATERS

In 2021, Martin Pirenne told Bravin and Damien that he was leaving Belgium.

Canada was calling. His girlfriend was studying there and Pirenne was keen to brew in a different environment. His two brewing partners understood. "Martin has three loves," says Damien. "His partner, La Jungle, and Montreal."

Bravin and Damien decided to continue together. But although La Jungle had attracted a fervent niche following, it was becoming difficult to penetrate the increasingly saturated beer market in their home city. Brussels was no longer the quiet brewing town it was when La Jungle's founders arrived at the end of the 2000s. Where there were just a handful of breweries

> "The beer is given time to fully express its wild side."
>
> — FÉLIX DAMIEN,
> BRASSERIE LA JUNGLE

then, now there were around 20 in the city. Independent bars in Brussels were also more interested in IPAs than session-strength Saisons. Urban drinkers didn't seem to go for pastoral beers.

La Jungle had launched in the midst of the COVID-19 crisis, and the slow recovery of the hospitality sector was hurting its sales. To make matters even more challenging, the war in Ukraine resulted in soaring prices for energy and raw materials, which meant La Jungle's margins were shrinking.

But despite losing one of its founders amid this wider disruption, La Jungle embraced its wild side. Bravin and Damien doubled down, followed their convictions, and produced a host of mixed-fermentation Saisons and Table Beers with fruit infusions like blood orange, white peach, and red plum. They labelled this new range of beers Sauvage, a French word meaning "wild."

IV.
SAUVAGE

La Jungle's plan for the future – shaped by what Damien describes as "a beer market slowing down and an uncertain global economic situation" – is to find a new home and focus specifically on its Sauvage range, the foundation of which is Bière de Table.

Martin Pirenne now brews at Toltèk Brasseur Artisan in Boucherville, Québec. He was back in Brussels in the summer of 2023, working alongside Bravin and Damien once more, this time on a La Jungle x Toltèk collaboration called Puesta de Sol: a wild Saison aged in Chardonnay barrels and macerated with cranberries.

Bravin and Damien also released a beer named after one of their favourite films. Délivrance is a Golden Ale with notes of jasmine, apricot, and orange marmalade, all built on top of a baked biscuit malt character. Its label is a colourful illustration from artist Fred Lebbe depicting three figures on a canoe, lost on a murky, ominous river, silhouetted against a red horizon. In the foreground, an arm emerges from the water. But it's not a shotgun it grasps. It's a bottle of La Jungle beer.

CUVÉE DEVILLÉ

*A Belgian Pale Ale that progresses like a piano concerto:
from the introductory, creamy mouthfeel to the soft, malty middle section,
and a flurry of fermentation notes in the finish*

Brett Pale Ale 6.2% ABV	**BROUWERIJ DEN HERBERG** O. de Kerchove d'Exaerdestr. 16 1501 Buizingen (Halle)	IBU: 36 EBC: 24

Hazy amber with a thick, foamy, white head | Graininess plus apple tart, mirabelle plum, and peach esters, with a hint of leather and wet hay | Fruity and spicy, and moderately dry, with a touch of acidity in the finish

INGREDIENTS

Buizingen municipal water

Pilsner malt, Pale Ale malt, Munich malt, Light Caramalt

East Kent Goldings, Hallertauer Mittelfrüher

Ester-forward Belgian ale yeast and a blend of Brettanomyces strains for conditioning

Dark candi sugar

DISCOVER

CAFÉ DEN HERBERG
O. de Kerchove d'Exaerdestr. 16
1501 Buizingen (Halle)

CAFÉ PADDENBROEK
Paddenbroekstraat 12
1755 Gooik

SCHOENTJES DRANKENSERVICE
Bergensesteenweg 747
1600 Sint-Pieters-Leeuw

RECOMMENDED FOOD PAIRING

Pork cheeks stewed in a tomato and Cuvée Devillé sauce

ABOUT THE BREWERY

Founded: 2008
Brew capacity: 18hl
Annual production: 1,800hl

OTHER BEERS PRODUCED BY THE BREWERY

Herberg Blond: Belgian Blonde Ale, 5.5% ABV

Herberg Tarwe: Witbier, 5% ABV

Herberg Tripel: Tripel, 8% ABV

Herberg Bruin: Belgian Dark Strong Ale, 9% ABV

Oude Geuze Devillé: Oude Geuze, 6.7% ABV

INSTRUMENTAL

Like being a musician, brewing requires years of dedication and solitary practice. Yet shared creative endeavours can sometimes be more fulfilling, especially when performed with family.

I.
ALLEGRO

Kloris Devillé always wanted to be a musician.

He learned to play his grandmother's French Pleyel piano, which had taken pride of place in the family home during his childhood.

In 2000, when he was 10 years old, he performed a piano concerto with his brother Akke Devillé, then 13, in the village's Church of Don Bosco. *Piano Concerto No. 10* was the only concerto that Wolfgang Amadeus Mozart wrote for two pianos, so that he could play the piece with his sister. The two young Devillé boys tackled it together, just as Mozart had intended with his own family.

While the boys practised, their parents, Bart Devillé and Ann Heremans (a construction worker and a teacher, respectively), attended a brewing course at the COOVI evening school in Anderlecht. Obsessed with the complex character of Orval Trappist Ale – a "wild" amber beer from the Abbaye Notre-Dame d'Orval in Belgium's Gaume region – they constructed their own 150l homebrew system. The couple longed to sell their beer in their own café, and years later, on 1 February 2007, they finally opened Café Den Herberg in Buizingen.

Propped up against the wall in the middle of this space, amid tall wax candles and large circular tables, was the piano on which Kloris Devillé had learned to play music. Devillé's brother and his five sisters helped in the bar when they could, but Kloris Devillé was accepted to study music at the Conservatoire Royale de Bruxelles, the most prestigious music school in Belgium.

Piano would be his full-time focus for five years, all day, every day. He was going to be a musician.

II.
ADAGIO

To fund his years of study at the conservatory, Devillé taught music on the weekends and began picking up shifts at the family café.

In 2008, the Devillés opened a small commercial brewery in a converted garage beside the café. Brouwerij Den Herberg brewed "clean" top-fermented ales, including a Blonde Ale, a Witbier, an Amber Ale, and a Brown Ale. Seeing his father and brother brew, Devillé began to take an interest in the production side of the business, and he even attended brewing classes on weekdays after music school.

Devillé's five years of study paid off. He nailed his final exam in 2012, when he played *Piano Concerto No. 1* in E-flat major by Franz Liszt, accompanied by his teacher, the famous Moldovan pianist Mikhaïl Faerman.

But after graduating, it became clear that musicians' contracts were thin on the ground. Symphony orchestras can require up to 30 violinists and 12 cellists, but only ever need one pianist. In addition, the long days of intense work at the conservatory and the many hours at the evening school had taken their toll. It was "'*teveel hooi op de vork,*' as we say in Flemish," says Devillé – "too much hay on the fork." He was tired of studying. He needed a break.

> "It was *'teveel hooi op de vork,'* as we say in Flemish – too much hay on the fork."
>
> — KLORIS DEVILLÉ,
> BROUWERIJ DEN HERBERG

On 1 September 2012, Devillé got on a plane to Australia with his girlfriend, Margo Cammue. They spent the next six months working on raspberry farms, making their way down the east coast from Cairns to Melbourne, on the other side of the world from his family's café and brewery.

III.

CRESCENDO

Nine months later, Devillé and Cammue returned home. His interest in brewing was still there, so in August 2013, he started working at Brasserie Timmermans in Itterbeek, which claims to be the oldest Lambic brewery in the world. At Timmermans, Devillé learned about complex sugars as opposed to simple ones, and about slow fermentations rather than fast ones.

Back in Buizingen, Devillé's father Bart and his brother Akke still harboured ambitions to brew a beer inspired by Orval, the Trappist beer fermented with the wild yeast Brettanomyces. But now that Kloris Devillé was gaining a more technical understanding of wild yeasts at Timmermans, they all agreed it was time to work together.

Brettanomyces – "British fungus" – is often seen as a contaminant in beer, the characteristics it imparts considered unwelcome "off-flavours." But the Devillés knew that, used as a "conditioning" yeast in combination with the right primary yeast, Brettanomyces could offer complex character, ranging from pineapple or apricot notes to more "interesting" flavours with barnyard or leather nuances.

Devillé and his family chose a characterful Saccharomyces yeast strain for primary fermentation of their new beer. The idea was that the fruity esters this yeast would produce – compounds such as isoamyl acetate (banana and peardrop), ethyl caprylate (apple), and phenylethyl acetate (roses, honey) – would help the Brettanomyces to create new, more complex flavours over time. "If your basic yeast is too clean, the Brettanomyces will express itself less," says Devillé.

But Brettanomyces is slow-acting and difficult to manage. The more sugars it eats, the more carbon dioxide it produces. The Devillés endured a frustrating period of trial and error, finding themselves with over-carbonated bottles which poured with ice-cream-like foam. They also had to be more diligent when cleaning tanks, the risk being that a small infection of Brettanomyces would render all their other beers "wild," and virtually impossible to package and sell.

After much tinkering and experimentation, the Devillés finally had a malty, fruity, and spicy Pale Ale conditioned with a wild yeast. They had created it together, as a family, working side by side. Before they could bring it to market, however, the beer needed a name.

IV.
CODA

The word *cuvée* derives from the French word *cuve*, meaning vat or tank, often used to refer to the best grape juice of a pressing or a batch of particularly high quality. In beer, it's generally used for the most desirable product from a brewery. The Devillés knew the Cuvée Devillé was their best beer. But they didn't know whether the Belgian public would agree.

The family presented the Cuvee Devillé for the first time publicly at the 2014 Zythos Bierfestival in Leuven. Word quickly spread around the event venue that a small family brewery from the Pajottenland was pouring an "Orval clone." Queues began forming at their stall. "We were surprised by the reaction," says Devillé.

Cuvée Devillé gave the family the confidence to pursue beers of even wilder character. In 2020, they released their first Oude Geuze, a blend of one-, two-, and three-year-old spontaneously fermented Lambics.

Kloris Devillé currently works at the breweries of the John Martin Group, including Timmermans, and now leads a new Lambic project at Bobbi Brewery in Ittre. But he's also more involved in the Devillé family brewery than ever before. "For me today, the main thing is to continue the family brewery," he says.

With three beer projects on the go, he doesn't often get time to play music anymore. But when his sister Fien plays the violin, he sometimes accompanies her on piano. He and Margo now have two young children – Sus, born in 2020, and Pie, born in 2022. When they're old enough, Devillé would like for them to play his grandmother's old brown Pleyel piano in the family café, while he enjoys a glass of Cuvée Devillé.

"If your basic yeast is too clean, the Brettanomyces will express itself less."

— KLORIS DEVILLÉ,
BROUWERIJ DEN HERBERG

LA MONEUSE

A semi-dry amber-coloured Saison with a honeyed, caramel maltiness and fermentation-forward fruit flavours of orange, peach, and apricot

| Strong Amber Saison 8% ABV | **BRASSERIE DE BLAUGIES** Rue de la Frontière 435 7370 Dour | IBU: 16 EBC: 18 |

Amber with white foam

Honey, peach, orange, and apricot

Caramel, citrus, and black pepper, with a semi-dry finish

INGREDIENTS

Spring water from a well

Pilsner malt, Munich malt

Saaz

A proprietary Belgian ale house yeast with a fruity ester profile

RECOMMENDED FOOD PAIRING

Wood-grilled fillet of beef at restaurant Le Fourquet

DISCOVER

LE FOURQUET
Rue de la Frontière 438
7370 Dour

LA MARELLE CAFÉ
Rue des Trieux 36
7040 Blaregnies

DRINK FACTORY
Chaussée du Roeulx 95
7000 Mons

ABOUT THE BREWERY

Founded: 1988
Brew capacity: 30hl
Annual production: 1,000hl

OTHER BEERS PRODUCED BY THE BREWERY

Bière Darbyste: Fig Saison, 5.8% ABV

Saison d'Épeautre: Spelt Saison, 6% ABV

La Vermontoise: Dry-hopped Spelt Saison, 6% ABV

La Moneuse Spéciale Winter Ale: Winter Ale, 8% ABV

La Moneuse Triple X: Strong Amber Saison, 10% ABV

BANDIT COUNTRY

La Moneuse is a deceptively simple beer. But just like the highway bandit after which it was named, there's more to it than you'd first imagine.

I.
MASSACRE

Brasserie de Blaugies is located on Rue de la Frontière (Border Street). It's named for the isolated Walloon townland in which it's located, a place where the fields, farms, and fences of Belgium intertwine with those of France. This border area has a history of lawlessness, and one of the brewery's beers – a Strong Amber Saison of 8% ABV called La Moneuse – is named after the region's most famous highway bandit.

Antoine-Joseph Moneuse is thought to have committed more than 20 assassinations and 160 thefts over the course of his infamous career. In the late 18th century, he terrorised mansions and robbed stagecoaches with his Chauffeurs du Nord highway gang. He and his loyal lieutenant, Nicolas-Joseph Gérin, reportedly tortured victims by burning their feet in the fireplace to elicit confessions as to where they had hidden their gold.

One of the most horrific atrocities Moneuse is accused of carrying out was the Massacre at the Auberge de La Houlette. On the night of 22 November 1795, nine people were murdered, including six children. Court documents mention bodies with wounds from multiple axe blows to the head, and a deceased 16-year-old girl who was found holding her dead baby sister in her arms.

The legacy of Moneuse lives on in this region. A well-known walking circuit encompasses key locations from the bandit's story. Local theatre groups perform reenactments of the massacre. There are even recipes online for Crêpe à la Moneuse, a pumpkin and apple pancake made with De Blaugies' beer.

However, the reason Brasserie de Blaugies named the beer La Moneuse is not only because he's a recognisable figure for locals – but because Antoine-Joseph Moneuse is family.

II.
FREE RISE

Kévin Carlier has been head brewer at De Blaugies since 2000, but he's been helping out at the brewery since he was 10 years old. His parents homebrewed in their garage and brewed their first commercial beer in 1988. Though Pierre-Alex Carlier and Marie-Noëlle Pourtois were teachers by trade, there was some brewing heritage in the family: Pierre-Alex's grandfather was a brewer. Kévin Carlier's early exposure to fermentation led him to study bioengineering at university.

La Moneuse was the first beer the family brewed. Carlier's mother, Marie-Noëlle Pourtois, says they based the beer on a recipe they found in the 1927 edition of "Larousse Ménager," an annual publication describing itself as the "Illustrated Dictionary of Domestic Life." With Carlier's bioengineering input, the beer evolved into what it is today: a fruity, full-bodied Saison with a bready, honeyed profile; a mild, earthy hop character; and fruity, peppery yeast notes.

Originally, De Blaugies sourced its yeast from the nearby Brasserie Dupont. But Carlier soon developed his own strain in a laboratory, and worked with Institut Meurice in Brussels on propagation and analysis.

> "Sinister bandit; execrated rascal; infamous thief of travellers delayed on the highways; shameless plunderer of isolated farms... odious brute whose nauseating memory still poisons resentful memories… Moneuse sows an irresistible terror behind him."
>
> — ALBERT JOTTRAND,
> AUTHOR OF *MONEUSE: UN CHEF DE BANDITS SOUS LE DIRECTOIRE*

While most ales are fermented in the range of 20°C to 22°C, De Blaugies' house yeast performs best in the 30s. "I put it in the fermentation tank at 32°C and block the temperature with cooling at 34°C," says Carlier. The result is an expression of fruity ester compounds which present with orange, peach, and apricot notes.

III.

DESCENDANT

If you ask Marie-Noëlle Pourtois how she feels about her family's brewery carrying the name of a murderer on its beers, she says that there's more to the story.

The familial connection to Moneuse is on her side. He had a relationship with his lieutenant's sister, Marie Thérèse Gérin, producing a son, Jean Baptiste. Moneuse was sentenced to death and beheaded by guillotine so he didn't get to know his child, but Jean Baptiste Gérin is a direct ancestor.

Citing the 1987 book *Moneuse*, written by Yves Vasseur, Pourtois claims that Moneuse did not commit the atrocities at the Auberge de la Houlette. She suggests that he targeted only the wealthy – large landowners, merchants, rich notaries – and that he gave some of the riches he stole to the poor, a kind of Walloon Robin Hood.

De Blaugies saw its own reputation grow fast in the 2000s. But its production capacity remained small. For Carlier, long days of intense manual labour produced just 7hl of beer from the family's tiny garage brewery. For 20 hours a day, he had to duck between the pipes, walls, and tanks of the cramped space to lift malt bags, untwine hoses, and manipulate valves. The cleaning, administrative, and sales tasks came when he was already exhausted. "It was too much," says his mother.

In 2010, Kévin Carlier suffered three heart attacks. He was just 32 years old. Nine stents were inserted into his arteries during emergency angioplasty procedures. It was clear that something at Brasserie de Blaugies would have to change.

IV.
LE FOURQUET

Carlier spent years designing a new, more automated brewing system that would maintain the integrity of the brewery's recipes while ensuring he could produce more beer with less strain. The family approached a bank and asked for support from the Walloon region, citing evidence of strong sales to secure the financing they needed.

The new brewery finally became operational in 2018. Carlier can now brew 30hl in one batch, and with the automated features of the new system, he can brew four batches in one day. The investment has changed the family's lives.

Today, 36 years after its creation, La Moneuse is still available to try at Le Fourquet, the family's restaurant located opposite the brewery. Lining its walls are framed illustrations by the famous Belgian artist Claude Renard. They depict scenes from the life of Moneuse: depictions of the massacre; of him giving a bag of riches to a poor woman; of him approaching the guillotine; of intimate scenes with his lover, Marie Thérèse Gérin.

The story of Moneuse is not what it at first seems. He grew up in a lawless place, following the invasion of the armies of the French Republic. He was a teenager when his father was murdered in a brawl and those in power had abandoned the people. He resorted to committing awful crimes to survive.

Kévin Carlier is no outlaw; there's no comparison between his experiences and those of his ancestor Moneuse. But his story is also not as it first seems. From the outside, people saw a carefree brewer in a tiny facility, living his family's dream. But Carlier too had to overcome circumstance – the small confines of De Blaugies' first brewery, financial restraints, and the limitations of his own body.

In the middle of the restaurant, there's a large circular grill, fixed with red brick and cement and several iron plates. Above the grill is a large extractor chimney made from shiny copper. Diners in the restaurant can watch their meat being grilled from their tables. If you ask Marie-Noëlle Pourtois if they've ever put anyone's feet in the fire, she answers without hesitation: "Only if they don't pay."

ARDENNE SAISON

A dry, bitter, fruity, and – if left long enough – slightly acidic Saison, refermented with Brettanomyces sourced from the skin of local Ardennes apples

Brett Saison
5.5% ABV

BRASSERIE MINNE
Zone d'Activités Nord 9
5377 Somme-Leuze

IBU: 40
EBC: 12

Slightly cloudy, deep gold, with a billowing white head

Citrus, earthy and floral aromas, and notes of hay

Dry, bitter, and slightly acidic

INGREDIENTS

Somme-Leuze municipal water, adjusted for pH and minerality

Pilsner malt, Pale Ale malt

Hallertau, Cascade, Warrior

Trappist ale yeast, Brettanomyces

RECOMMENDED FOOD PAIRING

Pot-roasted pheasant served with bread sauce

DISCOVER

BRASSERIE MINNE
Zone d'Activités Nord 9
5377 Somme-Leuze

PURA CEPA
Rue des Dolmens 3
6940 Durbuy

NOISEUX DELIFRAIS
Rue de l'Ourthe 36
5377 Somme-Leuze

ABOUT THE BREWERY

Founded: 2008
Brew capacity: 25hl
Annual production: 3,500hl

OTHER BEERS PRODUCED BY THE BREWERY

La Super Sanglier: Belgian Blonde Ale, 4.5% ABV

Ardenne Triple: Tripel, 8.5% ABV

Ardenne Stout: Imperial Stout, 8% ABV

Ardenne Belle d'Été: Witbier, 6% ABV

Ardenne Givrée: Winter Ale, 8% ABV

WILD BELGIUM

*Walloon engineer Philippe Minne made a beer to reflect
the wild nature of the mythical Ardennes forests. He hoped it would
help him grow his brewery as tall as the trees of his home region.*

I.

RAZORBACK

Philippe Minne grew up in the Ardennes, a region of extensive forests, rough terrain, and rolling hills. It lies primarily in the southeast of Wallonia, a dynamic and constantly changing ecosystem that boasts one of the highest forest growth rates in Europe. The Ardennes facilitated Wallonia's great industrial period, and its strategic position made it a centuries-long battleground for European powers.

As a child, Minne loved hearing mythical tales about the Ardennes. One story was about Arduinna, a goddess often represented as a huntress who rode a wild boar around the ancient forest. Another was about Trouffette, a mischievous elf who also rode a boar. Boars once flourished here, and they are still revered by local people for their symbolism of mystical forest life.

Philippe Minne was a civil engineer and electromechanic who produced machinery for steel plants. In his spare time, he enjoyed building things, especially old rally cars for racing events in the forests. But

he longed for more connection with the wildness of the Ardennes.

In 2008, Minne and his wife, Catherine Minne-Vanderwauwen, opened Brasserie de Bastogne as a side project, brewing on the weekends in a warehouse on a dairy farm in Vaux-sur-Sûre, 15km southwest of Bastogne. Their Trouffette range of classic Belgian ales showcased the folk character atop a boar, holding it by its razorback mane, her elvish ears poking out from a black, pointy hat as she galloped in full flight.

In its first year, Bastogne produced just 90hl of beer. The following year, demand increased and production doubled to 180hl. In 2011, it reached 400hl; in 2012, 570. Minne was ambitious. He hung up a bar chart in the warehouse detailing the annual production yield each year so he could see his progress – as if reminded by the forests of the Ardennes that mighty oaks from small acorns grow.

II.
THE MILKMAN'S SON

Phillippe Minne and Catherine Vanderwauwen met through a mutual friend when they were at university. In 1995, they went to the Pukkelpop music festival in Hasselt to see a joint performance by Canadian singer-songwriter Neil Young and American rock band Pearl Jam. Somewhere in between Young's hit *Big Green Country* and his encore that night, *Rockin' in the Free World*, they became a couple. "That was not our first meeting," says Minne-Vanderwauwen of the encounter that led to their marriage. "But that's when the flash happened."

Minne-Vanderwauwen was a city girl from Brussels, but she says that moving to the Ardennes with Minne was one of the best things she has ever done. In Brussels, the couple had ridden the Metro, lived in small

> "We really felt like we belonged with this movement and with the people."

— CATHERINE MINNE-VANDERWAUWEN,
BRASSERIE MINNE

spaces, and breathed city air. But in the Ardennes, they were surrounded by nature and would take long walks to talk about their plans for the future.

In the early 2000s, they discovered a new wave of Belgian breweries, such as Brouwerij De Ranke and Brasserie de la Senne, and began attending beer festivals. "We really felt like we belonged with this movement and with the people," says Minne-Vanderwauwen.

Minne started brewing in their garage. When his father, Paul Minne – a milkman and insurance broker – learned of his son's new pastime, he told stories about their family's brewing heritage. Philippe's grandfather, Jules Minne, had owned his own brewery nearby: Brasserie de Grand Leez. His great-grandfather, Joseph Minne, had brewed first in Brasserie Yproise in Ypres and then at Brasserie Val Saint Lambert in Seraing, just outside Liège.

Minne realised there was some part of his identity missing. Creating a beer that reflected the Ardennes wilderness was not just a flight of fancy. It was in his blood.

III.

APPLE SKINS

In October 2012, Minne hired Marc Cleeremans to help him create a *bière sauvage*, a wild beer to honour the Ardennes. Cleeremans was a young brewing engineer with a masters in agricultural science who had just completed a period of research on the brewing yeast at Brasserie de Rochefort. To endow their new beer with an unpredictable, untamed, and evolving character, Minne opted for a mixed fermentation. He would use both a top-fermenting Saccharomyces ale yeast and a wild yeast: Brettanomyces.

He secured the ale yeast from another nearby Trappist brewery – Brasserie d'Orval – which the Cistercian monks gave him at no cost. Minne and Cleeremans then sourced the wild Brettanomyces yeast from the skins of apples in an orchard 300 metres from the brewery. Cleeremans did tests on 20-litre batches to ascertain the flavour profile of the strain they had captured, and then sent it to the Institut Meurice in Brussels for storage and propagation.

They brewed the beer with Pilsner malt for a soft, grainy character and Pale Ale malt for biscuit notes, hopping with Hallertau, Belgian Cascade, and Warrior. Orval's ale yeast gave the beer a subdued fruitiness, with notes of peaches, lemons, and white grapes. The Brettanomyces was added pre-packaging, for refermentation in the bottle. In 2014, they released the beer as Ardenne Saison. On the label, three heavily tusked boars ran wild.

By 2017, Brasserie Bastogne's fast-paced growth was a problem. The brewery was cramped and stuck in an agricultural zone that offered no possibility of expansion. It had reached a production volume of 1,500hl per year. Minne had a choice: allow a lack of momentum to kill their project, or relocate the brewery and continue to grow. The latter option would require funds for a bigger facility. And they'd have to find a suitable location: Minne didn't want to leave the Ardennes.

IV.
SILHOUETTE

In 2018, Brasserie de Bastogne moved to an industrial estate in Baillonville, deeper into the heart of the Ardennes. With the help of a loan from the Société Wallonne du Crédit Social, they created a new home for their Ardennes beer. Cleeremans headed up production and Minne quit his engineering day job to oversee operations full-time. The brewery also changed its name to Brasserie Minne.

In addition to its Trouffette and Ardennes ranges, Brasserie Minne has added an Ardenne Wood range, named for both the forests that surround it and the fact that each of these new beers was aged in oak barrels. Their labels depict Ardennes wildlife: deer, foxes, owls, woodpeckers, magpies, beavers, pheasants, and wolves.

In 2023, the Brasserie Minne team produced 3,500hl at their new brewery. Minne says they could brew up to 10,000hl at their new facility with some investments. And they have no plans to stop growing.

Philippe Minne and Catherine Minne-Vanderwauwen still go for walks in the Ardennes forests today. They still listen to Neil Young together, including *Rockin' in the Free World*: a song about freedom, autonomy, and personal wildness. Minne is working on the restoration of an old rally car, which is wedged into the brewery storage space.

Their new building is a mighty oak compared to the acorn of those early days. The architecture of the building is strange, but intentional. It was designed to recreate a particular shape: the silhouette of a wild Ardennes boar.

Beer is an agricultural product, made with cereals such as barley, wheat, rye, spelt, and oats. These grains don't just give beer its colour, structure, and fermentable sugars – they impart flavours that range from biscuits, nuts, and toast to caramel, chocolate, and coffee. These are the *hidden beers* that will assassinate your cravings.

CEREAL KILLERS

FRANC BELGE

A biscuity, fruity, and bitter Spéciale Belge-style Pale Ale, which speaks to the elusive nature of Belgian identity and the steadfast values of its brewer

	BRASSERIE DE RANKE	
Spéciale Belge 5.2% ABV	Rue du Petit Tourcoing 1a 7711 Dottignies	IBU: 40 EBC: 20

Hazy amber with a frothy, off-white head	Biscuity malt notes and hints of peach esters with a floral, earthy hop aroma	Nutty and fruity with a firm, pleasant bitterness

INGREDIENTS

Dottignies municipal water

Pilsner malt, Pale Ale malt, Munich malt

Fuggles, Hallertau

A blend of two Belgian ale yeast strains

RECOMMENDED FOOD PAIRING

Beef carpaccio with Parmigiano Reggiano, pine nuts, rocket, and pesto

DISCOVER

TAPROOM DE RANKE
Rue du Petit Tourcoing 1a
7711 Dottignies
(Open Friday and Saturday)

SPÉCIALE BELGE TAPROOM
Regine Beerplein 1
2018 Antwerpen

HELLODRINK!
Boulevard d'Herseaux 85
7711 Dottignies

ABOUT THE BLENDERY

Founded: 1994
Brew capacity: 40hl
Annual production: 8,000hl

OTHER BEERS PRODUCED BY THE BREWERY

Guldenberg: Tripel, 8% ABV

XX Bitter: Belgian IPA, 6% ABV

Saison de Dottignies: Saison, 5.5% ABV

Noir de Dottignies: Belgian Strong Dark Ale, 8.5% ABV

Père Noël: Winter Ale, 7% ABV

HARD CURRENCY

*Franc Belge is a beer that celebrates the peculiar idea
of Belgian identity. It's produced by a brewery that personifies
the steadfast values, ruthless pragmatism, and understated excellence
of this small, strange nation.*

I.
IDENTITY

Brasserie De Ranke is a brewery which, in many ways, represents the incongruous, knotted, and multifarious nature of Belgian identity.

It's a Walloon brewery owned by Flemish brewers. It's located in Dottignies, a village in the Hainaut province of Wallonia. But its two co-owners, Nino Bacelle and his friend, Guido Devos, were born in Flanders and live in the Flemish towns of Wevelgem and Zwevegem, respectively. Workers at the brewery speak Flemish and French on a daily basis.

In 2018, in the face of polarising politics, Bacelle wanted to brew a new beer that could reignite a sense of unifying national pride. He wanted to name this new beer after a coin.

The Belgian one-franc coin – in circulation until Bacelle was 30 years old – was first issued just after the Second World War to symbolise a prosperous recovery.

"It's just a feeling," says Bacelle about using the one-franc coin on his new beer. "I wanted to express Belgian identity."

II.
SPÉCIALE

Nino Bacelle had only one beer style in mind.

Spéciale Belge was born from a competition in Liège in 1905. Belgian brewers were tasked with finding a beer that could compete with the growing volume of English ale and Bavarian lager imports into Belgium. The winner of the competition was Belge du Faleau of Brasserie Binard de Châtelineau, an amber-coloured ale with a biscuity malt profile, strong bitterness, and subtle yeast character: the first Spéciale Belge.

By the 1970s, Spéciale Belge was ubiquitous in Belgium. Bacelle recalls enjoying popular examples of the style such as Vieux Temps, Ginder Ale, Palm Spéciale, and De Koninck, all of which were malty, bitter, and hoppy. At that time, all were also produced by independent Belgian breweries. But everything changed in the late 1980s and early 1990s when family enterprises were bought by global conglomerates, and their beers' recipes transformed. "Everybody was making it sweeter and less hoppy," says Bacelle. "Everybody was changing the identity of this beer."

Today, Spéciale Belge is seen by many as outdated and boring. The beer style invented to celebrate Belgian identity seems to have become virtually irrelevant. "I was very well aware of the fact that it's not a beer that is popular anymore," says Bacelle. "But on the other hand, I don't want to see it disappear completely. When we made it, we went back to its roots, making it bitter again."

"It's just a feeling. I wanted to express Belgian identity."

— NINO BACELLE,
BRASSERIE DE RANKE

The version De Ranke created – named Franc Belge, after the Belgian Franc coin – was bready and a little nutty, built on a grain base of Pilsner, Pale Ale, and Munich malts. Bacelle fermented his amber-coloured ale with a blend of two Belgian ale yeasts, one with a pleasant apricot and peach expression and the other with subtle notes of banana, clove, and pepper. Most importantly, Bacelle used large quantities of Fuggle and Hallertau whole-cone hops, equipping the beer with a firm bitterness and an earthy, floral, and lightly spicy character.

But there was one catch. It was prohibited in Belgium to use the image and name of a national coin without the relevant permission of the national authorities. The only way De Ranke could use the likeness of the coin was to be granted permission by a representative of the Crown: specifically, the Mint Master at Brussels' Royal Mint of Belgium.

Without their consent, there would be no Franc Belge beer.

III.
MINT MASTER

On 16 November 2018, in the offices of the Royal Mint of Belgium, Giovanni Van de Velde – assistant to the Belgian Mint Master Ingrid Van Herzele – received Nino Bacelle's email request with the proposed label design featuring the Belgian one-franc coin.

"We have received your question," he responded by email six days later. "Our legal department is currently looking into whether this can be allowed." It was not unusual to receive requests for permission to refer to coins, but this was the first to come from a brewery.

When Van de Velde began examining De Ranke's proposed label design, he saw that the graphic was of the Belgian one-franc coin first issued in 1950. That particular coin was the most-minted in Belgium's history: 1.6 billion were produced between 1950 and 1988.

The 1950 Belgian one-franc coin was part of a trio of post-war coins: the 50-franc coin featured Mercury to represent aspirational trade; the 50-cent coin featured a miner and lamp to represent the rebuilding of industry; and the Belgian one-franc coin on De Ranke's label featured the head of Ceres, the goddess of grain crops, representing the hope of an agricultural revival. "They used those symbols for recovery, for the future, and for not looking back," says Van de Velde.

Ceres' head was a fitting symbol for a beer label. Van de Velde also noticed that the coin on the label featured both the words "België" and "Belgique," inclusive of the French- and Flemish-speaking communities living in the vicinity of the De Ranke brewery.

After checking the legal statutes, Van de Velde could find nothing to prohibit the use of the coin's image and name on a beer label. He composed another email to Nino Bacelle. "This one doesn't seem to be a problem," he wrote. "As a result, you can continue this wonderful initiative and launch it on the market. We are already looking forward to it."

> "Everybody was making it sweeter and less hoppy. Everybody was changing the identity of this beer."
>
> — NINO BACELLE, BRASSERIE DE RANKE

IV.
CIRCULATION

On 19 January 2019, Brasserie De Ranke launched its new beer, Franc Belge.

The launch event took place not at the brewery in Dottignies, but in the city that is most famous for Spéciale Belge today – Antwerp. The beer café chosen for the launch: Café Spéciale Belge.

"There's always a risk that the beer doesn't match with what you'd expect," says Giovanni Van de Velde. "But I was quite happy when I tasted the beer. It was good."

Around the same time that Franc Belge was released, the production facilities of the Royal Mint of Belgium were closed. The decision was taken for economical reasons. Production of Belgian coins is today carried out at the Royal Dutch Mint. It speaks to the ruthless pragmatism of Belgians, putting practicalities before national pride. "Why keep an organisation alive that is not completely efficient?" asks Van de Velde. There is, however, still a Mint Master of the Royal Mint of Belgium. Following the retirement of Ingrid Van Herzele, Giovanni Van de Velde was appointed to the role on 1 August 2022.

As for the 1950 Belgian one-franc coin, it lost its value on 1 January 2002 when the Euro became Belgium's official currency. But just like Spéciale Belge beers, ignored for so long, the coin lives on. Today in Belgium, old, unexchanged 1950 Belgian franc coins are wedged behind sofa cushions, lying under park bushes, and resting at the bottom of city fountains; 835 million of them. They are like the Belgian sense of identity – often hidden under the surface, but utterly distinct and stubbornly persistent.

TRIOMF

A smoked ale with flavours of sweet toffee, citrus, black pepper, and peat, produced by a Walloon family brewery for the 100th anniversary of a Ghent institution

Smoked Ale
6% ABV

BRASSERIE DUPONT
Rue Basse 5
7904 Leuze-en-Hainaut

IBU: 27
EBC: 20

Amber with
a frothy white head

Caramel, citrus,
and peated malt

Scotch fudge, stone fruit,
and black pepper, with a hint
of smoked meat

INGREDIENTS

Well water

Pilsner malt, Pale Ale malt, Abbey Malt, whisky malt (smoked during kilning with Scottish peat)

Two varieties of Hallertau hops

Dupont house yeast

RECOMMENDED FOOD PAIRING

Cheeseburgers prepared with
Dupont's Moinette cheese

DISCOVER

BRASSERIE DUPONT
Rue Basse 5
7904 Leuze-en-Hainaut
(bottle purchase only)

KUNSTENCENTRUM
VIERNULVIER VZW.
Vooruit Building
Sint-Pietersnieuwstraat 23
9000 Ghent

DRINK FACTORY
Chaussée du Roeulx 95
7000 Mons

ABOUT THE BREWERY

Founded: 1920
Brew capacity: 65hl
Annual production: 32,000hl

OTHER BEERS PRODUCED BY THE BREWERY

Moinette Blonde: Belgian Strong Golden Ale, 8.5% ABV

Avec Les Bons Vœux: Belgian Strong Golden Ale, 9.5% ABV

Saison Dupont: Saison, 6.5% ABV

Blanche du Hainaut Biologique: Witbier, 5.5% ABV

Monk's Stout: Belgian Stout, 5.2% ABV

ONWARD

Brasserie Dupont's Triomf is a triumph of trust forged through action, of innovation on the shoulders of generational legacy, and of two iconic institutions working together to create something extraordinary.

I.
SPECIAL MISSION

In 2012, Willie Verhoysen was approached with a special task.

Verhoysen was the hospitality manager at the Vooruit, a festival and arts centre housed in a grand building in the centre of Ghent. (*Vooruit* translates to "Onward.") At the time, Verhoysen had worked at the Vooruit for 28 years, 15 of those managing its kitchens, concert hall bars, restaurant, and café – one of the busiest hospitality venues in the city. "It's the salon of Ghent," says Verhoysen.

The Vooruit's Feestlokaal – its "Festivities Hall" building, located in Ghent's Sint-Pietersnieuwstraat – had been constructed in 1913 by the city's socialist cooperative, an architectural showpiece designed to give workers a cinema, library, and theatre hall, as well as a café and restaurant. The Vooruit had also constructed a cooperative brewery there, but unable to survive in the face of a radically changing beer market and in the aftermath of two devastating world wars, it closed in 1954.

1913 was also the year of the World Expo in Ghent, a huge trade fair and civic event that attracted nearly 10 million visitors to the city. The old Vooruit brewery had released a beer specifically for the occasion: a 4% ABV Blonde Ale called Triomf ("Triumph" in English). In its first year, Triomf was a hit, and made up two-thirds of the brewery's sales. Moreover, for the socialists, its name solidified their "triumph."

"The triumph was that the socialist movement would win the battle against the capitalists," says Willie Verhoysen of the beer's name. "That the working class would finally win, and there would be a new society – that there will be a complete triumph."

To mark the 100th anniversary of the Feestlokaal's construction, the Vooruit planned a whole year of festivities. As hospitality manager, Willie Verhoysen was tasked with a special mission: to produce a beer to celebrate the occasion. But he had less than 12 months to do it. The Vooruit no longer had a brewery of its own, so Verhoysen would have to find someone else to brew it.

II.
ORGANIC COLLABORATION

At the time, Verhoysen was working with large brewing company Alken-Maes for the majority of the Vooruit café's beers. He approached them about the project, but they weren't interested. "It was too small and special for them," says Verhoysen.

His next stop was Het Hinkelspel, a Ghent family cheesemaker that produced a Belgian ale called Lousberg, which Verhoysen sold as a local beer in the Vooruit café. But they were contracting their beers at another facility and were not in a position to assist.

Verhoysen then went to Hogeschool Gent, a higher education institution that offered courses in brewing science. They had their own brewing facility, but they didn't have capacity.

There was one more brewery left to contact. When Verhoysen had become hospitality manager at the Vooruit in 1997, he had wanted to include organic beers on the menu so that the venue could be a part of the solution to the world's growing environmental problems.

One of the few breweries producing organic beers at that time was a family brewery in the Walloon village of Tourpes called Brasserie Dupont. In the late 1990s,

"People said that it will cost you a few years to develop a very good beer. We didn't have the time."

— WILLIE VERHOYSEN,
FORMERLY OF VOORUIT

the Vooruit café started selling Dupont's organic beers. Verhoysen wondered if they would be interested in helping create the 2013 centenary beer. "People said that it will cost you a few years to develop a very good beer," says Verhoysen. "We didn't have the time." He had one more chance; one more hope of success.

III.
SMOKE SIGNAL

With the clock ticking down to the centenary celebrations, Verhoysen called Gust Simons, then the sales representative at Brasserie Dupont, to ask whether the brewery might be able to produce a special, one-off beer within a very quick time frame. Simons was enthusiastic, keen to create a Dupont beer for a respected Ghent institution like the Vooruit café.

But he would first have to convince Brasserie Dupont owner Olivier Dedeycker.

Dedeycker did not normally like special projects, and especially those that involved brewing for others, preferring instead to focus on his brewery's legacy brands, such as Saison Dupont and Moinette. Dedeycker is the fourth generation of his family to run Dupont, a former farm that dates back to 1759, and which started brewing in 1844.

To convince him, Simons took Dedeycker on a tour of the Vooruit building, "from the cellar to the top of the roof." He explained the history of the organisation and the vision for a centenary beer that would be organic and not too strong in alcohol. He also informed him that there was no time for tests. That tour "made him understand," says Simons, "...that it was kind of an honour."

Dedeycker opted for a Spéciale Belge, a beer style that came into prominence around the same time the Vooruit brewery created the original Triomf. But Dedeycker also decided to add a small amount of peated malt, and he fermented the beer with the expressive Dupont house yeast.

It was certainly a risk. Spéciale Belge had once been a popular beer style, but it had fallen out of favour in the 2000s, perceived by younger drinkers as boring and old-fashioned. In addition, the peated malt flavour proposed by Dedeycker might have proved divisive, as it does in beer styles such as Rauchbier and Smoked Porter.

But Willie Verhoysen and the Vooruit were running out of time. It was already the beginning of 2013. The beer was fermenting in tank and the labels had been printed. The second incarnation of Triomf was nigh.

IV.
THE SALON OF GHENT

In April 2013, Vooruit staff received bottles of the new beer. What they tasted was a dry, bitter, and fruity ale, certified organic, with a very soft, smoky touch. The malt flavours, thanks to Dupont's direct-fire heater, balanced Scotch fudge and sweet toffee notes with a refined peatiness, while the Dupont house yeast – typically fermented at higher temperatures to drive ester production – delivered what it has always given to the brewery's Saisons: esters of tangerine, peach, and passionfruit, with its subtle trademark black-pepper note.

The Vooruit staff loved it. "Everybody was convinced," says Verhoysen. "It's something special."

The general public in Ghent were similarly convinced. Such has been the success of Triomf that it's still being produced more than 10 years after it was commissioned as a one-off release. Brasserie Dupont kept brewing extra batches to meet demand, and today, Triomf is the second-best-selling beer at the Vooruit café, after only Maes Pils. It's poured in its own Saison-style *boerenglas* (farmer's glass), with "Triomf" spelled out in a bold, Art Deco, sans-serif font to match the original 1913 Triomf label.

Willie Veryhoysen retired in 2022. He still regularly pops back to visit old colleagues at the Vooruit café – now called VIERNULVIER ("Four-zero-four"). When he visits, he drinks the special beer he helped create: an organic Smoked Ale available only on draught in the majestic Feestlokaal building, produced by a Walloon family brewery for the triumphant 100th anniversary of an iconic Ghent institution.

SPECIAL EXTRA EXPORT STOUT

A full-bodied Foreign Extra Stout showcasing dark chocolate and espresso bitterness; notes of spice, liquorice, and hazelnut; and a background lactic sourness

Foreign Extra Stout 9% ABV	**DE DOLLE BROUWERS** Roeselarestraat 12b 8600 Diksmuide	IBU: 50 EBC: 90
 Dark black with an off-white, almost beige head	 Liquorice, coffee, chocolate, and hazelnut	 Dark chocolate and espresso flavours, with a tart finish

INGREDIENTS

Local well water

Pilsner malt, Special B malt, three different roasted barley malts (900, 1200, 1400)

Nugget

Ale yeast, Lactobacillus

RECOMMENDED FOOD PAIRING

Oysters served on the half shell with lemon wedges, Tabasco sauce, and mignonette

DISCOVER

DE DOLLE BROUWERS
Roeselarestraat 12b
8600 Diksmuide
(Open Saturday and Sunday)

'T BRUGS BEERTJE
Kemelstraat 5
8000 Bruges

DRANKEN VANDEWOUDE
Monnikshoekstraat 22
8630 Veurne

ABOUT THE BREWERY

Founded: 1980
Brew capacity: 30hl
Annual production: 1,200hl

OTHER BEERS PRODUCED BY THE BREWERY

Oerbier: Belgian Strong Dark Ale, 9% ABV

Arabier: Belgian Strong Golden Ale, 8% ABV

Boskeun: Belgian Strong Golden Ale, 9% ABV

Dulle Teve: Tripel, 10% ABV

Stille Nacht: Belgian Strong Golden Ale, 12% ABV

WET AND STRONG

Few brewers in Belgium are as wildly playful in showcasing their personality as Kristiaan Marie Boniface Herteleer of De Dolle Brouwers.

I.
HOSPITAL BREWERY

Kristiaan Marie Boniface Herteleer, better known as Kris Herteleer, had his first encounter with Stout in 1970, at the age of 15, when his brother Ward broke his leg.

Their family doctor recommended that Ward drink two Stouts a week to recover, specifically a sweet Milk Stout imported from England called Whitbread Extra Stout. A local merchant who delivered beer suggested the brothers try another Stout that was brewed in Ireland but was bottled in Antwerp: an 8% ABV Foreign Extra Stout called Guinness Special Export.

Foreign Extra Stout is a dark, strong, dry, well-hopped, and roasty beer that would have originally been exported from Britain to its 18th-century colonies in Africa, Asia, and the Caribbean. Herteleer was attracted to the style's history, learning that foeder-aged versions of the beer would have presented with a slight lactic sourness in 19th-century London. He was charmed by Guinness Special Export's distinctive flavour and iconic branding.

A few years later, Herteleer learned that Guinness brewed beer in a facility in London, more easily reachable from northwest Belgium than Guinness' home in Dublin, Ireland. So he wrote a letter to ask whether he could visit. The reply came shortly afterwards: Make the trip.

The Guinness brewery in Park Royal, London was not as Kris Herteleer had imagined it. "It was all white walls, sterile tiles, and glass," says Herteleer. "I came to see a brewery but instead I'd seen a hospital." Herteleer wanted the brewery to be artful; to have charisma. Instead it was sanitised of all personality.

But there was one thing during the visit that Herteleer did like: The sales manager who received him had "nice shoes, and a bow tie."

II.
COSTENOBLE

Herteleer's first experience with brewing was when another brother, Jo, returned from London with medical books and a homebrew kit.

Kris and Jo Herteleer began brewing beer in a copper vessel designed for washing laundry using the supplied malt extract, hop powder, and dry yeast. Unimpressed by their initial results, they started sourcing real ingredients closer to home: malt and hops produced locally in the Westhoek region, and yeast collected directly from Rodenbach, famous for its Flemish sour beers.

In the meantime, Herteleer was expressing his personality through architectural drawings, sketches, and painted portraits. He brought these sketches and portraits to parties to show friends, parties at which they'd also showcase their beers. At one such party, Herteleer and his brother met Romeo Bostoen, a local investor, and after tasting the beers together, the trio began looking for a brewery. Their first visit was to Brouwerij Costenoble in Esen.

What they saw on that day in 1980 was a beat-up brewery dating back to 1835 in a village of 2,000 inhabitants. "The brewer told us that it would be sold that afternoon to another guy," says Herteleer. "But that guy never showed up. So we told him to sell it to us at the same price. We bought it there and then."

The Costenoble brewery was not a "hospital" brewery of "white walls, sterile tiles, and glass." It was a maze of nooks and crannies and ladders, with a gravity-filled coolship; traditional open-air Baudelot cooler; and deep, open, copper fermentation baths. It was a brewery for artisans. It was a brewery with personality.

> "I came to see a brewery
> but instead I'd seen a hospital."
>
> — KRIS HERTELEER,
> DE DOLLE BROUWERS

III.
EXPORT

Within two years of buying Brouwerij Costenoble, Kris Herteleer and his brother bought out Bostoen and upscaled the mechanical efficiency of the system. They named the enterprise De Dolle Brouwers (The Mad Brewers). Later, when Jo Herteleer moved to South America to practise medicine, Kris Herteeler was left to brew and manage the brewery himself.

Over the decade that followed, Herteleer began producing Strong Belgian Ales such as Oerbier (9% ABV), Arabier (8% ABV), and Stille Nacht (12% ABV), all of which combined pronounced malt profiles, fruity yeast character, and a hint of lactic sourness procured from the Rodenbach yeast.

One fortuitous day in 1990, Herteleer received a call from his U.S. importer, Matthias Neidhart of B. United International Inc. Could De Dolle Brouwers brew a Foreign Export Stout for the United States? Herteleer hadn't brewed one yet because it was a difficult style to sell in Belgium: Local drinkers were accustomed to versions that veered into Belgian Dark Strong Ale territory, with their sweeter finishes and spicier yeast profiles. But now the request had come directly. Herteleer said yes.

His grain bill for this intense, full-malt beer included Pilsner malt for biscuit notes and fermentable sugars, Special B malt for a touch of caramel and toffee, and three grades of roasted barley malt for chocolate and coffee flavours. A bittering addition of Nugget would provide a subtle woody backbone.

Herteleer mashed – without sparging – in his 19th-century cast iron tun, before pulling the wort through both a copper coolship and the Baudelot cooler to ferment in deep, open fermentation baths. He believes this gives the beer a distinct "softness." Because copper is so porous, it also allows the lactic acid bacteria of the Rodenbach yeast to garnish the beer with a tartness, making it reminiscent of the original foeder stouts of 19th-century London.

The result – De Dolle Special Extra Export Stout – was a beer of unquestionable charm.

IV.

OERBIERMAN

Today, 69-year-old Kris Herteleer brews at De Dolle Brouwers with his protegé, Lennart Pynebrouck, who grew up next door to the brewery in Esen. Herteleer's wife, Els Herteleer, assists in the bar and balances the brewery's books. Their 24-year-old son, Boniface Herteleer, is studying both brewing and accounting, primed for involvement in the family business.

Over the years, the brewery has been infused with Herteleer's artistic charm. Above the cave-like brewery bar is an artist's workshop, filled with hundreds of tubes of acrylic paint. On one wall hang the calendars he has made every year since the early 1980s. Another wall showcases watercolour portraits he paints every year of Butter Knights, local people who have been inducted into the Orde van de Beuterwaeghe – The Order of Butter Weighing – which celebrates butter production in the area.

All over the brewery are representations of Oerbierman, the Michelin Man-esque yeast cell cartoon character which Herteleer created as the brewery's mascot. On weekends, Herteleer gives tours of his antiquated brewery, always dressed in a yellow Oerbierman jacket, pointy purple and turquoise shoes, and a colourful bow tie. Above the front entrance to the brewery, there's a massive depiction of Oerbierman, himself wearing a red bow tie.

The brewery's motto – *Nat en Straf* ("Wet and Strong") – appears on its signage, out front, on the delivery van, and on its glassware. "Wet" references beer, of course, but also the sweat-drenched endeavour of brewing. "Strong," as well as speaking to the flavour intensity and alcohol content of Herteleer's beers, also refers to the strength of his personality. Everyone needs to find their bow tie.

VICARIS WINTER

A spiced Winter Ale with notes of dark red fruits; burnt caramel; hints of tobacco and aniseed; and a boozy, spicy finish

| Winter Ale
10% ABV | **BROUWERIJ DILEWYNS**
Industrieterrein Hoogveld
Vlassenhout 5
9200 Dendermonde | IBU: 34
EBC: 84 |

| Dark reddish-brown with an off-white head | Dark fruits and burnt caramel, with hints of tobacco and chocolate | Fruity and malty, with a moderate sweetness, full body, and a warming finish |

INGREDIENTS

Dendermonde municipal water

Pilsner malt, caramel malt, roasted barley malt

Two varieties of German noble hops

Abbey-style ale yeast

Sugar

Liquorice and star anise

DISCOVER

BROUWERIJ DILEWYNS
Industrieterrein Hoogveld
Vlassenhout 5
9200 Dendermonde
(Visits by reservation)

IN DE POEPEKAS
Dijkstraat 120
9200 Dendermonde

DRANKENCENTRALE MAES
Hoogveld 29
9200 Dendermonde

RECOMMENDED FOOD PAIRING

Flemish beef stew

ABOUT THE BREWERY

Founded: 2005 (company); 2010 (brewery)
Brew capacity: 25hl
Annual production: 4,000hl

OTHER BEERS PRODUCED BY THE BREWERY

Vicaris NANO°: Alcohol-Free Blonde Ale, 0.3% ABV

Vicaris Lino: Flax Blonde Ale, 6.5% ABV

Vicaris Tripel: Tripel, 8.5% ABV

Vicaris Generaal: Belgian Strong Dark Ale, 8.5% ABV

Vicaris Tripel/Gueuze: Tripel and Lambic Blend, 7% ABV

DARK HORSE

As a child, Claire Dilewyns was excluded from a major honour in her city. But the brewery and beer she created with her father and sisters would become the pride of Dendermonde.

I.
1990

On 27 May 1990, four boys – decked out in full armour and carrying swords and shields – were paraded around their hometown astride a giant model horse six metres high, two metres wide, and five metres long. The horse's head was a wooden sculpture dating back to the 1600s, decorated with ostrich feathers and festooned in the red and white colours of the city. Its black tail was fashioned from the hair of 30 living horses.

It was the centrepiece of the Dendermonde Ommegang, a procession that takes place once every 10 years. The spectacle celebrates the legend of the Ros Beiaard: a magical horse, known for its strength and intelligence, and said to have carried the Four Sons of Aymon as they fled from emperor Charlemagne.

The four boys atop the horse were the Veldeman brothers: Gert, Stijn, Stefaan, and Toon. They were selected against strict criteria: They had to be four consecutive brothers, without a girl in between; all born and living in Dendermonde; whose parents and grandparents were born in Dendermonde; and aged between seven and 21 years old on the day of the procession. The Veldemans were treated like heroes by the spectators, who cheered and celebrated with beers in hand.

Claire Dilewyns was born in Dendermonde three days later. She, too, has three siblings: Anne-Cathérine, Julie, and Hélène. But together, they are four sisters – and the rules dictate that only brothers can ever ride the horse. Claire Dilewyns would never be able to serve Dendermonde at the Ommegang.

II.
2000

Two days short of her 10th birthday, Claire watched her very first Ommegang. Roy, Nick, Ken, and Dean Coppieters were the brothers selected to ride the Ros Beiaard in 2000. Claire watched them soak in the adulation.

At the time, she was helping her dental technician father with his newfound hobby of homebrewing. Vincent Dilewyns had brewed his first beer on 11 December 1999 in his garage. Together with her sisters, Claire assisted in bottling beers and cleaning equipment. Bit by bit, she learned about the technical processes of mashing, fermentation, and packaging.

Vincent Dilewyns' first beer was named Vicaris Tripel, a reference to his name ("Vi" for Vincent) and to his profession (*cariës* refers to tooth decay). The name was also a hint at the inspiration Vincent took from the Trappists (*vicaris* means "vicar" in Flemish).

First, there was a small batch for Anne-Cathérine's communion party. Then another for a local historical society exhibition. Vincent arranged that a larger batch be brewed under licence at contract facility De Proefbrouwerij, 25 kilometres away in Lochristi. Then in 2006, the Dilewyns were invited to the Zythos Bierfestival in Sint Niklaas, where Vicaris Tripel won the Zythos Consumer Trophy for the beer most appreciated by festival attendees.

Before long, the Dilewyns had beer distributors, retailers, and enthusiasts showing up at their front door, all seeking out Vicaris Tripel. "We received thousands of

"Vicaris: Vi *(Vincent)* + cariës *(tooth decay)*"

people in buses from all over the country," says Claire. "It was the start of something new and big for us as a family."

After the Vicaris Tripel came Vicaris Generaal, a Belgian Dark Strong Ale of 8.5% ABV named for Dilewyns' wife, Genevieve Leysen – the "general" of the family. The third beer was Vicaris Tripel/Gueuze, an innovative blend of the Tripel with Lambic from a Pajottenland producer.

Like the Ros Beiaard Ommegang, their fourth beer was seasonal. Vicaris Winter is a spiced Winter Ale brewed once every year, in July, so that it has time to ferment and condition appropriately for release in October. It's a boozy beer of 10% ABV with a roasty, caramel-like malt character, red-fruit esters, and hints of liquorice and star anise. By the time the Dilewyns released Vicaris Winter, their side project had exploded.

> "It was the start of something new and big for us as a family."
>
> — CLAIRE DILEWYNS,
> BROUWERIJ DILEWYNS

III.

2010

As the next group of Dendermonde brothers – Maarten, Niels, Dieter, and Michiel Van Damme – prepared to mount the Ros Beiaard horse in 2010, the Dilewyns were mounting up for an adventure of their own.

Two of Vincent Dilewyns' daughters decided to start a commercial brewery with their father: Anne-Cathérine would work in production; Claire in marketing, accounting, and sales. The youngest sister, Hélène, studied biochemistry, and would potentially join the brewery in the future. Julie would go on to work in customer care engineering, but as a trained chef she would also help out with catering at brewery events.

In March 2010, the Dilewyns installed their new brewing system in the Hoogveld industrial estate in Dendermonde, where flax was historically processed.

At one of the first hospitality trade expositions that the family attended, they arrived late to the event and struggled to erect their stand. A young man named Kristof Bastiaens offered to help. He worked for the Barry Callebaut Group of chocolate producers that were also exhibiting at the exposition. Vincent invited Bastiaens to the Dilewyns' stall for a beer, where he met Claire. Today, the couple are married with two children.

In 2017, Anne-Cathérine Dilewyns decided that she wanted to pursue other projects and left the brewery. Vincent Dilewyns planned to retire. And so Claire Dilewyns became the head of Dendermonde's only brewery.

IV.
2020

The Dendermonde Ros Beiaard Ommegang of 2020 could not take place due to the COVID-19 pandemic, so the four selected brothers – Marteen, Wout, Stan, and Lander Cassiman – did not get to ride the horse until May 2022. For this edition, Brouwerij Dilewyns brewed the official beer of the Ommegang, named simply Ros Beiaard. Attendees cheered while holding Vicaris beers in their hands.

In 2022, Kristof Bastiaens quit his job as sales director at the Barry Callebaut Group to work full-time alongside his wife as co-owner of Brouwerij Dilewyns.

Just as Vincent strove for innovation, so too do Claire Dilewyns and Kristof Bastiaens. Vicaris Lino is a Blonde Ale of 6.5% ABV infused with flax fibres, which the brewery describes as "the first beer in the world brewed with flax." Vicaris NANO° is an alcohol-free lager. All of Brouwerij Dilewyns' beers are produced today as Vincent preferred – without filtration, centrifugation, or pasteurisation.

No one knows what the next Ros Beiaard Ommegang in Dendermonde, scheduled for 2030, will bring for Brouwerij Dilewyns. The couple's children, Juliette and Leonie, will never be selected to ride the Ros Beiaard, just as Claire Dilewyns never made it onto the horse. But she's left her mark on the town. The brewery she owns and runs produces beers which have become an integral part not only of the decennial Ommegang celebrations, but of the life of the city in the years in between.

A symbol has appeared on the brewery logo of Brouwerij Dilewyns since the beginning, and still appears on every bottle and glass from the brewery today. It's a depiction of a horse, carrying four people on its back. The outline of their clothes and the way their hair flows wildly in the wind suggest that the four sisters did get to ride the horse after all.

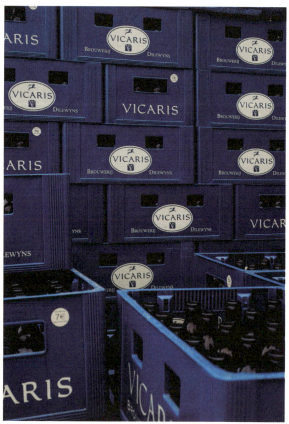

Belgian brewers often meld a respect for tradition with playful experimentation. These are the *hidden beers* that deploy out-of-the ordinary ingredients or processes to produce revelatory drinking experiences.

UNUSUAL SUSPECTS

WHITE GOLD

A Tripel produced with the roots of the witloof (Belgian endive), an ingredient that offers a soft, lingering bitterness, as well as a window into the agricultural origins of the resilient family who brews with it

Witloof Tripel 8% ABV	**BROUWERIJ HOF TEN DORMAAL** Caubergstraat 2 3150 Tildonk	IBU*: 30 EBC*: 14
 Dark orange and hazy	 Banana, herbal, grassy	 A bready malt backbone with notes of banana, citrus, and black pepper, finishing with a lingering, balanced bitterness

INGREDIENTS

Well water with a hard profile

Pilsner malt, raw wheat

Magnum, Hersbrucker

Hof ten Dormaal house yeast

Roasted Belgian endive roots

RECOMMENDED FOOD PAIRING

Belgian endive rolled in slices of ham and covered in a creamy cheese sauce (*hespenrolletjes*)

DISCOVER

HOF TEN DORMAAL
Caubergstraat 2
3150 Tildonk
(Open Saturday)

DE RECTOR
Oude Markt 4
3000 Leuven

HOPS 'N MORE
Parijsstraat 27
3000 Leuven

ABOUT THE BLENDERY

Founded: 2009
Brew capacity: 25hl
Annual production: 1,200hl

OTHER BEERS PRODUCED BY THE BREWERY

Saison: Saison, 5.8% ABV

Bouts: Witbier, 4.5% ABV

Tripel: Tripel, 8% ABV

Tinto: Belgian Blonde, 6% ABV

Zure van Tildonk: Flemish Sour, 6% ABV

*Colour and bitterness depend on how intensely the Belgian endive has been roasted (the longer and hotter the roast, the darker and more bitter the result).

TAKING ROOT

Witloof – also known as Belgian endive, or chicory – has the same qualities as the Janssens family who own Hof ten Dormaal: grounded, stubborn, and remarkably resilient.

I.
NEW FRONTIER

In 2007, Jef Janssens' father suffered a stroke. André Janssens had lived a stressful life as an accountant, but now the family was sent spinning in a new direction. "I lost everything," says André. "My business. My potential. My joy for life."

Following his recovery, André took a month-long trip abroad to find himself, flying to the Rocky Mountains in Montana. When André returned from Butte, a former copper boomtown, he told Jef that he had brought back a 15hl brewery.

André believed brewing to be a "stressless life." "Monks brew and they live until they're a hundred," he thought at the time. André and his wife Mol sold their house in Kampenhout and moved Jef and his brother and sister to the Hof ten Dormaal farmstead in Tildonk, a picturesque rural property built in the 1150s which required more than a little work to refurbish. It wasn't until the brewing equipment arrived that André realised he didn't know how to use it. He didn't know how to brew. In fact, he didn't know anything about beer.

André got his sons, Jef and Dries, involved. Eventually, Jef would become the brewer, developing at first a classic trifecta of Belgian ales: Blonde, Amber, and Dark. It was a good start, but the range inspired neither Jef nor Hof ten Dormaal's early consumers.

They decided to stick it out and created a fourth beer – one which would be a riskier commercial choice in a conservative beer market, but would more truthfully speak to their newfound farming identity, and to the agricultural heritage of their homeland.

II.
WHITE LEAF

White Gold is a Tripel brewed with the roots of the *witloof*, a vegetable known in English as chicory or Belgian endive.

The beer was built on the base of a classic Tripel. Jef sourced a yeast from local brewing consultant Filip Delvaux, a strain marrying the banana and apricot character of a Belgian ale yeast and the peppery notes and deep attenuation of a Saison strain. It's brewed using barley grown on the Hof ten Dormaal farm and then malted at the Dingemans family maltery in Stabroek. Twenty percent of the beer's grain bill is raw wheat, also from the farm, while the Magnum and Hersbrucker hops used are harvested by the family every September.

The white gold reference demonstrates the high regard for *witloof* in Belgium, where it was discovered in 1834. *Witloof*'s heartland is Flemish Brabant, and more specifically, the town of Kampenhout – the Janssens' original home.

Witloof – literally "white leaf" – is a unique vegetable in appearance, a torpedo head of tightly packed white leaves. When raw, it is crisp and bitter. When cooked, its sharper flavours soften into a mellow, nutty sweetness.

Jef Janssens began sourcing *witloof* for his beer from a farmer in Kampenhout, and used the root of the plant rather than the white leaves, roasting it and adding during the boil. "It gives a more soft, smoother, rolling bitterness that lingers way longer than hop bitterness does," says Jef.

But working with *witloof* as an ingredient in beer is not easy. It's difficult to dial in consistent levels of bitterness – much depends on the length of time the *witloof* root is roasted, and at which particular temperature.

The vegetable itself is also challenging and labour-intensive to cultivate. Unlike most other vegetables, each *witloof* has to be planted and grown twice: first in the field, to extract the root from the seed; and second in a warehouse or under a canvas, to "force" the root under cover of complete darkness to develop its distinctive pointed cigar shape.

But *witloof* is an incredibly hardy vegetable. It's tolerant to cold temperatures, not particularly vulnerable to diseases or pests, and can grow in soils of varying nutrient compositions. *Witloof* is resilient. *Witloof* will always try to find a way.

III.
BURNT

Early in the morning of 6 January 2015, Jef Janssens was woken by rubble falling outside his bedroom window.

A fire had broken out in the red-brick farm hall where the brewery was installed. The chimney of the warm chamber, used to referment beers, had caught alight.

The Janssens family sprang out of bed and called the fire brigade immediately, but by the time the fire was extinguished, it had completely destroyed the roof of the brewery, the entire bottling line, the conditioning rooms, and most of the brewery's stock.

Soon afterwards, the Janssens family learned that the insurance company would require an investigation, meaning a long, drawn-out claim before they could get funds to replace the roof. "It's like any disaster," says Jef. "The first week, everybody is there to pick you up. But people have their own lives to live. There comes a time, very fast, when you're left on your own."

For three years, Jef worked in the brewery without a roof, brewing in the cold and rain and wind, constantly moving boxes of bottles around under tarpaulin so they wouldn't be destroyed. At times, the weather was so bad they had to rent temporary shelter. In addition, they lost several quality mechanisms because of the fire, including their glycol cooling line, and so had less control over fermentation temperatures. "Quality-wise and sales-wise, we crashed down hard," says Jef.

IV.
INNOVATION

When the insurance funds finally arrived, the family was able to rebuild the roof, but the years of hardship, and some self-admitted financial naivety, meant that their business continued to struggle.

But then, Hof ten Dormaal was chosen to appear on the TV show *Andermans zaken* ("*Other people's business*") in which host Kamal Kharmach helps entrepreneurs who are facing an urgent problem. Through scrupulous examination of their financials and focusing only on their core products, one of which was White Gold, Hof ten Dormaal earned the opportunity in October 2023 to pitch to Delhaize, one of the country's biggest supermarkets. Delhaize was impressed by Jef Janssen's

"From the outside, we look like a hippy commune."

— JEF JANSSENS,
BROUWERIJ HOF TEN DORMAAL

pitch and by Hof ten Dormaal's story and product, and its beers were listed in 800 stores around Belgium, transforming the prospects of the farm brewery.

Today, in addition to a family brewery, the Janssens grow six hectares of cereal, cultivate hops, and raise livestock on their ecological farm. Jef's parents, brother, sister, and their respective partners and children work together to overcome hardship. "From the outside, we look like a hippy commune," he says.

Every year since the fire, Hof ten Dormaal has organised the Leuven Innovation Beer Festival. It takes place at De Hoorn, the historic brewhouse in which Stella Artois was created for the very first time in 1926.

Before every edition of the festival, the attending brewers are invited to a brunch at the Hof ten Dormaal farm. The brewers stand together under the new roof of the small taproom, sharing their ideas while drinking a beer made from *witloof* by a family who just doesn't know how to quit.

THÉORÈME DE L'EMPEREUR

A Pale Ale produced with green tea and jasmine flowers that combines perceived floral sweetness, cracker and cereal maltiness, and a tropical-fruit hop character

| Jasmine and Green Tea Pale Ale
6.4% ABV | **BRASSERIE DE L'ERMITAGE**
Rue Lambert Crickx 26
1070 Anderlecht | IBU: 30
EBC: 8 |

 Hazy gold with a lively, white foam

 Floral, herbal, and citrusy, with tropical fruit aromas

 Candied sweetness, perfume, oranges, grapefruit

INGREDIENTS

 Brussels municipal water

 Pilsner malt, Pale Ale malt, Vienna malt

 Columbus, Ekuanot

 American ale yeast

 Double infusion with green tea and jasmine

DISCOVER

BRASSERIE DE L'ERMITAGE
Rue Lambert Crickx 26
1070 Anderlecht

L'ERMITAGE SAINT-GILLES
Rue de Moscou 34
1060 Saint-Gilles

LES CAVES DE L'ERMITAGE
Rue Gheude 53
1070 Anderlecht

RECOMMENDED FOOD PAIRING

Orange-blossom-honey-glazed chicken with crispy potatoes

ABOUT THE BREWERY

Founded: 2017
Brew capacity: 8hl
Annual production: 1,800hl

OTHER BEERS PRODUCED BY THE BREWERY

Lanterne: American-Style Pale Ale, 5.5% ABV

Noire du Midi: Porter, 6.9% ABV

Soleil: American Wheat Ale, 4.5% ABV

Holy Mountain: Dry-Hopped Sour, 3.8% ABV

PLAYING YOUR CARDS RIGHT

Nacim Menu is inspired by the avant-garde work of filmmaker Alejandro Jodorowsky, whose style was informed by a lifelong study of tarot. In setting out to become the Jodorowsky of Belgian brewers, Menu discovered the power of symbology.

I.
JODOROWSKY

An emperor on a toilet throne made of two intersecting dolphins.

This was Spanish Surrealist artist Salvador Dalí's condition for accepting the role of the Emperor in Alejandro Jodorowsky's failed adaptation of science fiction novel *Dune* in the late 1970s. Jodorowsky agreed to give Dalí the toilet throne and a hefty fee of $100,000 per hour to act in the movie, but planned to film the artist for only one hour, with the rest of his lines to be spoken by a robotic lookalike. Unsurprisingly, Jodorowsky's wildly over-budget 14-hour-long script was never made.

Nacim Menu was a film student in Brussels when he fell in love with the work of Jodorowsky, including films like *The Holy Mountain*, *El Topo*, and *Poesía Sin Fin*. In 2010, he even travelled to Paris to try to find the director in Café Le Téméraire, a café where he had been rumoured to give tarot readings. "He's like the pope of tarot," says Menu, referring to the tarot symbology in Jodorowsky's films.

"I fell in love with the symbolism and the mystery around it."

— NACIM MENU,
BRASSERIE DE L'ERMITAGE

Tarot is a deck of playing cards with symbols and narratives that can spark conversations, inspire ideas, and reveal new perspectives. Menu's mother Nacira had introduced him to tarot when he was young. Later, Menu had tattooed his body with tarot symbols (he has The World tattooed on his forearm and The Star tattooed on his thigh). He collected special tarot decks from all around the world. "I fell in love with the symbolism and the mystery around it," says Menu. "Not as a fortune-telling object, but more as a way of seeing the world around us and learning about ourselves."

In the end, Menu never met Jodorowsky. But he was inspired by the director's focus on tarot as a tool for creativity.

II.
THE HERMITAGE

In Brussels, Menu was living in an apartment block on the Rue de l'Ermitage in Brussels' Ixelles district. The co-living space became a burgeoning community of artists, musicians, and culinary creatives during the 2010s. It was known as L'Ermitage – the Hermitage.

The community would drink tea together and discuss tarot, art, films, music, food, and drinks. The fresh tea leaves they used were purchased from a shop close to the Hermitage, La Septième Tasse. Menu's choice of tea was often a green tea with jasmine flowers, which he loved for its earthy flavour and floral sweetness.

At the Hermitage, Menu met Mons native Henri Bensaria and Brusseleir François Simon. At first the trio shared cooking tips. Then they signed up for a wine education class. Eventually, they opened a commercial brewery together in 2017, naming it after their Hermitage community.

Brasserie de l'Ermitage is located in an old cigarette packing depot on the Rue Lambert Crickx. The founders based its aesthetic on tarot, in particular on the card of The Hermit, an old man standing on a mountain peak carrying a lit lantern with a six-pointed star.

Lanterne became their flagship beer: an American-style Pale Ale of 5.5% ABV, its label featuring a depiction of The Hermit, designed in Jodorowsky-inspired graphic colour. Soleil, their Wheat Ale, was based on the tarot card of The Sun. They hung artistic interpretations of tarot cards all over the walls of the brewery, including The Fool, The Moon, The Hanged Man, and The Star. They even hosted tarot readings in their taproom.

The logo of the brewery would be The Hermit's "lamp of truth," a lantern used to guide the unknowing, helping to navigate the road to enlightenment. "It's kind of a light at the end of a tunnel," says Simon. "For us three, it was the beginning of a new journey."

III.
TEA PARTY

Menu, Bensaria, and Simon wanted to produce a beer that reminded them of their tea-drinking days at the Hermitage community in Ixelles.

L'Ermitage's Pale Ale infused with green tea and jasmine was originally named Théorème de Li Chun-feng after the Chinese mathematician, and because it matched the name of the tea brand they were using, Jasmin Chun Feng.

But when that tea producer in China had a bad harvest, they embarked on a tasting with La Septième Tasse to find a replacement. "Now, we are going for one of the most expensive," says Menu. "It's very strong, so we can use less, so at the end of the day, it's about the same amount of money. But it's very important to have good quality."

With their new tea in hand, the founders decided to change the name of the beer to Théorème de l'Empereur: Theorem of the Emperor. Its branding is based on The Emperor tarot card.

The beer is brewed with Pilsner malt, Pale Ale malt, and Vienna malt for a biscuity profile, and is fermented with a clean American ale yeast. Green tea and jasmine are added as a double infusion, packed into muslin hop bags at a rate of half a gram per litre, and lowered into the beer during boiling and then again for 24 hours into tanks during fermentation.

The green tea gives the beer a grassy note, and the jasmine flowers offer a subtle sweetness and floral quality. This is complemented by the use of Ekuanot hops, which enhance the floral, grassy, and fruity flavours. "The idea with the green tea and jasmine is to feel it,

to smell it," says Bensaria. "But it should stay a beer … not as something in between."

IV.
THE EMPEROR

In tarot, The Emperor is an old man commonly depicted sitting on a ram-adorned throne wearing long robes and holding a sceptre. He symbolises power and ego; the dominance of logic over emotion; mind over heart. The card seemed to be a statement of L'Ermitage's aspiration for success. However, an alternative reading of The Emperor is one of structure: That you can pursue your creative goals in a similar fashion to The Emperor – methodically, rigidly, strategically.

As Brasserie de l'Ermitage has matured – it turned seven in the summer of 2024 – it has also become more focused and more disciplined. Gone are the crazy parties the founders used to throw at the Hermitage, the beer festival attendances every weekend, the unending iterations and collaborations. Menu is a father now, and so his business is no longer just an adventure with his friends; he must provide for his family.

Despite the fact that, as a tea and flower beer, Théorème de l'Empereur risks being niche, it has become one of L'Ermitage's best-selling beers out of the 220 brands or so it has produced to date, second only to Lanterne. On the online beer-rating website Untappd, it is L'Ermitage's highest-rated beer.

Jodorowsky's *Dune* movie was never made, and a robotic Salvador Dalí was never seen as his Emperor. But Nacim Menu's Emperor rules on emphatically. Menu and his team have built systems and processes at their brewery to ensure their creative goals are accomplished, no matter how abstract those ambitions are.

ADELHEID

A rich, malty Barleywine infused with oak chips that have been soaked in apple cider distillate from the Haspengouw region

Oaked Calvados Barleywine
10% ABV

BROUWERIJ DE HOPHEMEL
Bampslaan 21
3500 Hasselt

IBU: 46
EBC: 31

Dark amber with a slight haze and off-white head

Dried red fruit, green apple, vanilla, and caramel

Spicy and richly malty, with an oaky, boozy finish

INGREDIENTS

Hasselt municipal water

Pilsner malt, Pale Ale malt, light crystal malt, Special B malt, rye malt

Magnum, Citra

Abbey ale yeast

Dark candi sugar

Oak chips soaked in *appelstook* distillate (from Het Aerts Paradijs of Beringen)

DISCOVER

BROUWERIJ DE HOPHEMEL
Bampslaan 21
3500 Hasselt

BOTTLO
Schrijnwerkersstraat 21
3500 Hasselt

MARLOU DRANKEN
Heikensstraat 11
3520 Zonhoven

RECOMMENDED FOOD PAIRING

Hasseltse speculaas cookies from the bakery BAKKERSDOCHTER
Minderbroedersstraat 32
3500 Hasselt

ABOUT THE BREWERY

Founded: 2020 as cuckoo brewers; 2023 with own brewery
Blending capacity: 10hl
Annual production: 350hl

OTHER BEERS PRODUCED BY THE BREWERY

Hiëronymus: West Coast IPA, 6.5% ABV

Alexandra: DDH NE IPA, 5.8% ABV

Joannes: Hoppy Pale Ale, 5.5% ABV

IN PERSPECTIVE

Belgium's Haspengouw is an agricultural region some consider a beer wasteland. The owners of Brouwerij De HopHemel set out to prove it could be a beer heaven.

I.
WASTELAND

When Steven Broekx and Geert Vandormael met in 2012, they shared the same frustration. Sitting beside each other at a beer appreciation course in Hasselt, they lamented the lack of diversity in their region's beer scene. Broekx was an architect; Vandormael a logistics officer at the East Limburg Hospital. The pair became close friends, and hatched a plan to shake things up by creating uncommon styles that showcased local ingredients and flavours.

The Haspengouw is a loamy plateau between the Meuse and Scheldt rivers whose cultural heartland is in Limburg, south of Hasselt. Back in 2012, it wasn't highly regarded for its beer scene. Its fertile soil and gently rolling slopes were better suited to growing fruit than grain, and its inhabitants were an agricultural people with classic tastes: Brouwerij Alken-Maes' Cristal Pils, Brouwerij Wilderen's Tripel Kanunnik, and Brouwerij Kerkom's Bink Blond.

At the time, the local beer scene seemed to be falling apart. Brouwerij Amburon in Tongeren had just declared bankruptcy. The longstanding local beer club, the Limburgse Biervrienden (Limburg Beer Friends), ceased its activities for good, unable to recruit new, younger members. According to a beer importer from the region, Kristof Tack, "Haspengouw is a bit of a beer wasteland." Steven Broekx and Geert Vandormael set out to prove otherwise.

II.
THE *DRUIVELAAR*

When they began brewing in 2017, in a barn in Zepperen, Broekx and Vandormael had plenty of inspiration for beer concepts – a Pinot Noir Brut IPA, a Mirabelle Berliner Weisse, a Thai-spiced Russian Imperial Stout – but they didn't know what to call their creations. Then they noticed the *Druivelaar*: a tear-off, one-page-per-day calendar that has been ubiquitous in Flemish homes since the early 1900s.

The *Druivelaar* features different saints for each day of the year. "It's a never-ending source of names," says Broekx, who began to see it not just as a traditional calendar but as a marketing tool. Their Imperial Maple Syrup Stout became Hilarius; their Beetroot Sour IPA Gildas; their Raspberry Hibiscus Saison Rumoldus. The name of their project followed the celestial theme: They called themselves De HopHemel (The Hop Heaven).

Broekx and Vandormael started hosting intimate beer-and-food-pairing events, but it was a challenge to bring even the most basic new ideas to locals. Vandormael had to explain what an IPA was every day. Broekx had to justify why brewers worked with cans rather than bottles. But the events quickly sold out, and garnered them a reputation for interesting beers and a novel approach. They produced bigger batches at Brouwerij Den Toetëlèr in nearby Hoeselt and then at the BRAUW facility in Genk.

By 2019, following demand from cafés, restaurants, and distributors, they planned to open their own commercial brewery.

And then, coronavirus.

"Haspengouw is a bit of a beer wasteland."

— KRISTOF TACK,
GOBSMACK BEER IMPORTER

Not only were Broekx and Vandormael unable to brew together during the lockdown, but their day jobs became especially demanding.

As an architect focusing on residential properties, Broekx was busier than ever as people invested in their spaces. In the East Limburg Hospital, Vandormael became responsible for delivering hundreds of pallets of masks, gloves, and protective clothing. The newfound challenge gave them purpose. But it also gave them perspective: They should go after the things that mattered to them.

III.

APPELSTOOK

The pair officially incorporated Brouwerij De HopHemel in October 2020, and opened their Hasselt taproom in November 2022. Their brewery – a 10hl system with four 10hl fermenters – became operational in December 2023.

One of their beers was a Barleywine, a style that few, if any, locals had tried. They used light crystal and Special B malts for chewiness and complexity, as well as rye for added spiciness, body, and foam stability. Belgian abbey yeast delivered flavours of pepper, raisins, and plums.

But Broekx and Vandormael wanted to add a Haspengouw element. They soaked oak chips in a local, Calvados-like apple cider distillate, *appelstook*, produced by a nearby brewery and distillery, and infused them into the beer with a hop gun for a touch of green apple and vanilla. The result was a rich, full-bodied beer with a fruity, port-like character. "We want to be a little experimental," says Vandormael. "I think what we're doing is unique here."

As they turned to the *Druivelaar* to find a name for the beer, they saw the date they'd brewed it – 16 December 2022 – was dedicated to Adelheid, known in English as Saint Adelaide of Burgundy. Adelheid was one of the most important female rulers of her time, and made a major contribution to the expansion of the Holy Roman Empire. She showed a male-dominated

"We want to be a little experimental.
I think what we're doing is unique here."

— GEERT VANDORMAEL,
BROUWERIJ DE HOPHEMEL

medieval society a new vision of women in power. Broekx and Vandormael would use Adelheid to give people in the Haspengouw a new perspective on beer: its flavours and aromas; how it could be produced differently; how it could reflect the place they lived.

Adelheid became one of HopHemel's most popular beers. With its *appelstook* infusion, it spoke to the region's tradition of fruit-growing and distillation. Its pleasant sweetness and spice appealed to lovers of classic Tripels, but it also showcased enough complexity to intrigue the most particular of beer enthusiasts.

IV.
"READING BETWEEN THE LINES"

In recent years, the Haspengouw beer scene has blossomed. Chef Raf Sainte works regularly with Broekx and Vandormael to deliver beer-and-food-pairing events at his award-winning restaurant, De Gebrande Winning. Raf Souvereyns, owner of the Hasselt-based Lambic blendery Bokke, regularly brings friends and clients to HopHemel's taproom; it also pours beers from Hoptwins Brouwers, Boes Brewing Company, and other local producers. The activity in HopHemel's taproom gives the impression that this beer community is a new one, but these people were all working in beer long before Steven Broekx and Geert Vandormael encountered them.

Broekx often goes cycling with his family to other villages in the Haspengouw. They regularly visit an art installation, "Reading Between the Lines," an impressive, church-like sculpture made of steel plates. It's designed so viewers can see the landscape through the plates no matter where they stand, but what they see depends on their position.

As an architect, Broekx enjoys finding the spots where he is hardly able to see the church at all, as if the construction had dissolved into the landscape. From other viewpoints, however, the church is completely visible, its walls and roof dominating the surrounding orchards.

When he started out in beer, Broekx couldn't see anything that excited him locally. But since then, his perspective has changed. The people that are driving the Haspengouw beer scene have always been there. You just needed to be in the right place to see them. When you move one step to the side, a whole new perspective can appear right in front of you.

DE VLIER BRUT

A dry, floral-fruity, slightly acidic, and highly carbonated beer, produced with lager yeast, Lactobacillus, and homemade elderflower syrup

Apéritif Beer 8% ABV	**BROUWERIJ DE VLIER** Leuvensebaan 219 3220 Holsbeek	IBU: 5 EBC: 9

Pale blonde with a spritzy head | Lemon, apple, bergamot, and grass-like notes | Dry, floral, fruity, and highly carbonated

INGREDIENTS

Holsbeek municipal water

Pilsner malt, wheat malt, oat flakes

Lubelski

Lager yeast, Lactobacillus, Champagne yeast

Homemade elderflower syrup

DISCOVER

BROUWERIJ DE VLIER
Leuvensebaan 219
3220 Holsbeek
(Open Saturday)

CAFÉ APERO
Oude Markt 52
3000 Leuven

HOPS 'N MORE
Parijsstraat 27
3000 Leuven

RECOMMENDED FOOD PAIRING

Honey garlic shrimp

ABOUT THE BREWERY

Founded: 2008
Brew capacity: 5hl
Annual production: 250hl

OTHER BEERS PRODUCED BY THE BREWERY

De Vlier Demi Sec: Semi-Dry Apéritif Beer, 8% ABV

De Vlier Rosé: Rosé Apéritif Beer, 8% ABV

De Vlier Blond: Belgian Blonde Ale, 7.5% ABV

De Vlier Scotch: Scotch Ale, 8% ABV

Smokin' Elder: Smoked Ale, 8.5% ABV

FLOWER POWER

Engineers invent. They solve problems. When brewing engineer Marc Andries faced beer sceptics in his taproom at Brouwerij De Vlier, he turned to an unusual ingredient for the solution.

I.
SPARKLING IDEA

Marc Andries had a problem. In 2009, he was confronted by visitors to Brouwerij De Vlier's small taproom who refused to try any of his beers. Andries endeavoured to cater for all tastes, but this crowd couldn't be convinced. They just didn't like beer.

Marc Andries owns De Vlier along with his stepdaughter Karen Schuyten. The name of the brewery comes from Vlierbeek, the suburb of Leuven in which it was founded in 2008. It started in a café known as Bieduif'ke, itself named for the popular Flemish sport of pigeon racing (the reason a pigeon appears on the brewery logo). In 2009, for logistical reasons, Andries moved the brewery to a detached house in Holsbeek.

Andries studied chemical engineering and agricultural biotechnology at Vrije Universiteit Brussels and worked for brewery system manufacturers, aerospace companies, and solar power providers. Before starting his own brewery, he began as a brewing engineer at Brasserie d'Achouffe and Brouwerij Haacht. Alongside De Vlier, Andries has worked for 15 years for Belgosuc, a company that provides speciality sugars for the brewing and food industry.

Engineers invent. They solve problems. Andries sought out a way to convert the non-beer lovers in De Vlier's tasting room. "If you go to a party, everybody drinks sparkling wine," he says. If he could just convince people who believed they didn't like beer to try one that tasted like sparkling wine, he could challenge their perception of what beer could be. If they liked it, it might be a gateway to other beers in his range.

Andries set out to create a beer that tasted like a brut sparkling wine: dry, fruity, slightly acidic, and highly carbonated. It would be an apéritif beer to open the palates and minds of beer sceptics in his taproom. And he would do it using a specific ingredient: elderflowers.

II.
ELDERS

Brut is a term reserved for the driest of a producer's bottles. Many of the existing Belgian brut beers were produced according to the *méthode traditionnelle*, a process during which bottles undergo *remuage* (turning and shaking to move the lees into the neck) and *dégorgement* (the removal of those lees) before they're dosed with a *liqueur d'expédition* (a mixture of wine and sugar, to encourage secondary fermentation) and then corked and caged.

But for Marc Andries, beers produced in this way were still too much like beer rather than sparkling wine. "If you want to convince somebody who doesn't like beer to drink it, then you have to really go away from the beer taste," he says.

Andries knew there was a man living in the street behind his mother's house in the village of Bunsbeek who grew fruit trees and wild elders. The elderflowers were highly fragrant, with a green and sweetly floral scent and refreshing undertones of citrus, apple, and grass. "Elderflower gives some fruity-flowery flavours which you also find in Champagne," says Andries.

"Elderflower gives some fruity-flowery flavour which you also find in Champagne."

— MARC ANDRIES,
BROUWERIJ DE VLIER

The elder tree blooms in late May. Its flowers are creamy-coloured; its trunk short; its bark grey-brown, furrowed, and corky. It's sometimes referred to as the "Judas tree" as Judas Iscariot is said to have hanged himself from an elder. Some cultures believe that burning the elder brings bad luck; others recommend planting one by your house to keep the Devil away.

The elder is prominent in popular culture, too: the elder wand in the final book of the Harry Potter series; Elton John's 1973 track *Elderberry Wine*; and John Cleese's famous line as the French Taunter in *Monty Python and the Holy Grail*: "Your mother was a hamster, and your father smelt of elderberries."

III.
BRUT OF A BEER

In his brewhouse, Andries made a 1:1 syrup of sugar and water. He added wild elderflowers, 1kg for every 20l of syrup, and left them for an hour and a half so that their aromas and flavours were infused in the sugar solution. He then filtered and boiled it so it was sterile for brewing.

De Vlier Brut is brewed with Pilsner malt for simple sugars and crisp flavours; wheat malt for a citrusy, almost tart touch; and oat flakes for a robust body and velvety mouthfeel. Andries uses a lager yeast strain for primary fermentation to mimic the clean fermentation flavours of sparkling wine. "Lager yeast doesn't make as many esters as an ale yeast," he explains.

Andries also pitches a house strain of wild Lactobacillus, which he attained initially by doing open fermentations in his brewery. These lactic acid bacteria get to work during bottle conditioning to produce a clean acidity in the beer. As hop compounds hinder the development of lactic acid bacteria, Andries hops very conservatively with Lubelski, a Polish aroma hop variety with distinct herbal flavours and notes of cinnamon, bergamot, and lemon.

Importantly, Andries doses the beer right before bottling with his homemade elderflower syrup and a Champagne yeast. This sparks a secondary fermentation, which increases the carbonation of the beer to sparkling-wine levels, as well as infusing it with the floral and fruity notes of the elderflower.

> "If you go to a party, everybody drinks sparkling wine."
>
> — MARC ANDRIES,
> BROUWERIJ DE VLIER

IV.
BRINGING COLOUR

Today, Andries and Schuyten and their families pick elderflowers in late May or early June from the wild elder trees behind Andries' mother's house. When pushed for the exact location, Andries smiles. "It's a secret," he says.

De Vlier Brut is now the brewery's best-selling beer. It's been so successful at converting those nonbelievers in De Vlier's taproom that it's spawned three additional *apéritif* beers. After De Vlier Brut came De Vlier Demi Sec, a slightly sweeter version with more elderflower syrup.

The third instalment – De Vlier Rosé – was initially produced using raspberries, but the colour dissipated quickly. They couldn't sell a rosé beer that wasn't rosé in colour, so they tried Schaarbeekse cherries, which held their colour for longer. However, after a time the cherry compounds began sedimenting in the bottom of the bottle.

Always the engineer, Andries found the solution once more in the elder tree. The current version of De Vlier Rosé is made from cherries, but also elderberries, the small dark-red fruit that appears in late summer and autumn once the elderflowers have been pollinated by insects. Elderberries add a beautiful, stable rosé colour to beer and are both sweet and tart, tasting like tangy, earthy versions of blackberries.

It's perhaps a coincidence given the prominent role that the tree has played in the brewery's creative identity, but its name could not be more aptly chosen. It was called De Vlier because it was first established in the village of Vlierbeek. But in Dutch, De Vlier translates as "The Elder Tree."

To help you continue your tasting adventures, I've compiled an additional selection of *Hidden Beers of Belgium* to seek out. For the following list, I've been more relaxed about the rules of curation set out at the beginning of the book for the purposes of greater inclusion and discovery.

MORE HIDDEN BEERS

THIRST CRUSHERS

Low-alcohol and easy-drinking

BAVIK SUPER PILS (PILSNER, 5.2% ABV)
BROUWERIJ DE BRABANDERE
Rijksweg 33, 8531 Bavikhove
An unpasteurised Pilsner brewed by a West Flemish family brewery with 100% Pilsner malt, noble hops, and cold conditioning of at least 30 days.

ESTIVALE (BELGIAN PALE ALE, 5.2% ABV)
BRASSERIE ARTISANALE DE RULLES
Rue Maurice Grévisse 36, 6724 Rulles (Habay)
A hoppy, dry, and fruity Pale Ale from one of the most important independent breweries in Belgium.

EXTRA 4 (PATERSBIER, 4.8% ABV)
BROUWERIJ ST. BERNARDUS
Trappistenweg 23, 8978 Watou
A zesty, dry, and refreshing lower-alcohol abbey-style ale, whose recipe was resurrected from the period when this family brewery was licensed to brew for the Trappists of Westvleteren.

HOPPY MADAME (WITBIER, 4.5% ABV)
EN STOEMELINGS
Rue Dieudonné Lefèvre 37, 1020 Brussels
A dry and bitter Witbier hopped with Aramis and Strisselspalt from a brewery whose name translates to "in secret" or "on the sly."

IN DE NAAM VAN DE ZOON: CUSTODIA
(AMPHORA SOUR, 4.5% ABV)
HEILIG HART BROUWERIJ
Brusselsesteenweg 85A, 9230 Kwatrecht
A dry, vinous, woody beer fermented with yoghurt and sourdough culture, matured in oak barrels and ceramic amphora containers, and then blended in a brewery located in the Heilig Hart Kerk (Holy Heart Church).

KEREL GRAPEFRUIT IPA (FRUITED IPA, 4.5% ABV)
VBDCK BREWERY
Antwerpsesteenweg 12, 9140 Tielrode
A fruited IPA produced with grapefruit purée from the De Cock family of charcuterie fame, who in 2015 renovated the old Verbeeck-Back village brewery in Tielrode which operated between 1867 and 1966.

PICO BELLO (NON-ALCOHOLIC IPA, 0.3% ABV)
BRUSSELS BEER PROJECT
Rue Antoine Dansaert 188, 1000 Brussels
A refreshing and fruity Hazy IPA (featuring Amarillo, Citra, and Ekuanot hops) finishing with a subtle acidity, billed by the brewery as "the first Belgian alcohol-free craft beer."

ÜMLAÜTS ÜNLEASHED (KÖLSCH, 5.5% ABV)
TIPSY TRIBE BREWERY & DISTILLERY
Chaussée de Jette 374, 1081 Koekelberg
A grainy, bright, dry, and thirst-quenching Brussels interpretation of the Cologne beer style Kölsch, named playfully for the German diacritical mark.

VENUS EFFECT (GOSE, 4.5% ABV)
BRASSERIE SURRÉALISTE
Place du Nouveau Marché aux Grains 23, 1000 Brussels
A sour, salty, and piney interpretation of the Gose style, from a Brussels brewery located in an old banana warehouse with impressive Art Deco architecture.

VICHTENAAR (OUD BRUIN/FLEMISH RED, 5.1% ABV)
BROUWERIJ VERHAEGHE
Sint-Dierikserf 1, 8570 Vichte
A traditional Flemish red-brown beer of mixed fermentation, matured in oak casks for a minimum of eight months and blended to achieve notes of green apple, red fruit, and wood.

ACID TEST

Wild, complex, and full of zing

CUVÉE SAINT-GILLOISE (LAMBIC BLEND, 5% ABV)
BRASSERIE CANTILLON
Rue Gheude 56, 1070 Anderlecht
A two-year old Lambic dry-hopped with Styrian Goldings, brewed first to celebrate the 2003–2004 Division III title win and promotion for the Royale Union Saint-Gilloise football team.

CUVÉE SOEUR'ISE (FRUITED SOUR, 8% ABV)
BROUWERIJ DE LEITE
De Leiteweg 32, 8020 Ruddervoorde
A semi-dry, tart, blood-red fruit beer, produced by macerating De Leite's Tripel for six months on *cerises* (cherries) at a ratio of 250g of sour, unpitted cherries per one litre of beer.

GUEUZE GIRARDIN 1882 BLACK LABEL (GEUZE, 5% ABV)
BROUWERIJ GIRARDIN
Lindenberg 10, 1700 Sint-Ulriks-Kapelle
A traditional Geuze with lemon and grapefruit notes from one of the unsung heroes of Belgian beer.

JUICY & WILD RHUB-ELLE (FRUIT LAMBIC, 5% ABV)
LAMBIEK FABRIEK
Eugène Ghijsstraat 71, 1600 Sint-Pieters-Leeuw
A crisp, fruity, tart, and dry blend of Lambics matured with rhubarb from an exciting Pajottenland brewery that ironically describes itself as the "Fabriek" ("Factory").

KRIEK MARIAGE PARFAIT (CHERRY LAMBIC, 8% ABV)
BROUWERIJ BOON
Fonteinstraat 65, 1502 Halle
A rich cherry Lambic with hints of vanilla and cloves, produced by the Boon Lambic dynasty, made with 400 grams per litre of overripe cherries and aged in smaller oak barrels.

OUDE GEUZE CUVÉE ARMAND & GASTON (OUDE GEUZE, 5.5% ABV)
BROUWERIJ 3 FONTEINEN
Molenstraat 47, 1651 Lot
A blend of one-, two-, and three-year-old Lambics brewed at 3 Fonteinen with notes of citrus, green apple, white grape, and oak, and named in honour of founder Armand Debelder and his father Gaston.

OUDE GEUZE DE CAM (OUDE GEUZE, 6% ABV)
GEUZESTEKERIJ DE CAM
Dorpsstraat 67, 1755 Gooik
A dry, slightly bitter, and softly acidic Geuze, produced by a purist of the Lambic world who plays the *doedelzak* (Flemish bagpipes).

PLUCHE (FRUIT LAMBIC, 6% ABV)
BOFKONT
Mechelsesteenweg 340, 2250 Kontich
A blend of one-, two-, and three-year-old Lambics matured with white peaches and riesling grapes from a blendery named after the owner's childhood stuffed dog toy.

STEENGAARD (FRUIT LAMBIC, 6% ABV)
BOKKE
Maastrichterstraat 5/301, 3500 Hasselt
A blend of Lambics matured with apricots, white peaches, würzer grapes, and white muscat grapes from a Limburger who playfully describes his blending techniques as in accordance with the fictional Méthode Goat.

VANDERVELDEN 135 OUDE GEUZE VIEILLE (OUDE GEUZE, 6.5% ABV)
OUD BEERSEL
Laarheidestraat 230, 1650 Beersel
A *malse* blend of Lambic matured in Tuscan Brunello di Montalcino and Oud Beersel foeders, created as a tribute to Henri Vandervelden, who founded Oud Beersel in 1882.

WOLF PACK

Expressing the howl of the hop

BRUSSELEIR (BLACK IPA, 8% ABV)
BRASSERIE DE LA SENNE
Anna Bochdreef 19/21, 1000 Brussels
A complex, dry, and fruity Black IPA – or is it a hoppy dark Saison? – from one of Belgium's best and most influential breweries.

CARPE (SESSION IPA, 4.7% ABV)
LA SOURCE BEER CO.
Rue Dieudonné Lefèvre 4, 1020 Brussels
Named for the carp river fish, this is a juicy IPA with notes of peaches, passionfruit, and mango, from a Brussels brewpub leading the way in Belgium for hoppy beers.

HOPNYTIZED NEW ENGLAND IPA (HAZY IPA, 8% ABV)
ENIGMA
Schreverland 22, 3550 Heusden-Zolder
A juicy IPA, double-dry-hopped with Mosaic and Citra, from a small brewery that likes to bring colour to their labels.

HYPNOTIZE (DDH COLD IPA, 6.6% ABV)
DIAZ BREWING COMPANY
Rue du Canard 01, 7331 Baudour
A dry, aromatic, and fruity Cold IPA, produced by an American-Belgian husband-and-wife team in a small-scale facility located in the middle of a Walloon forest.

MY FAVOURITE SCAR, YOU KNOW WHO YOU ARE
(HAZY IPA, 6.1% ABV)
UNCHARTED BREW CO.
Oudaan 15/W28-29, 2000 Antwerp
A Hazy IPA dry-hopped with Mosaic and Idaho 7, produced by a brewpub in the centre of Antwerp which merged two up-and-coming Antwerp brewing entities.

RENINGE BITTER BLOND (BELGIAN BLONDE ALE, 7% ABV)
SEIZOENSBROUWERIJ VANDEWALLE
Zwartestraat 43, 8647 Lo-Reninge
A characterful, earthy ale produced by a city archivist in his nano brewery, made with coriander seeds and hops from Poperinge.

SABRO (IPA, 5.2% ABV)
TOURETTE BREWING
Vredestraat 1, 9050 Gentbrugge
A fruity IPA brewed with barley and wheat malt, dry-hopped with Sabro Cryo Hops for aromas and flavours of lemon and mint, and fermented with a Kveik yeast for notes of tangerine.

SMASHINE (PALE ALE, 6.3% ABV)
COHOP
Chaussée de Wavre 950, 1040 Etterbeek
An amber-coloured Pale Ale showcasing the pink grapefruit and dried rose notes of the Talus hop, and produced by Brussels' first cooperative brewery.

TROUBADOUR MAGMA (TRIPEL IPA, 9% ABV)
BROUWERIJ THE MUSKETEERS
Reepstraat 208, 9170 Sint-Gillis-Waas
A combination of a Belgian Tripel and a Double IPA, this fruity, spicy, and bitter beer was one of the first in Belgium to combine Belgian yeast, American hops, and high alcohol.

URINE (DOUBLE IPA, 7% ABV)
BRASSERIE DU BORINAGE
Rue François Dorzée 99, 7300 Boussu
A big, fruity IPA brewed with Citra and Amarillo Cryo Hops by a cooperative Walloon brewery that likes to experiment with ingredients.

FUNGUS KINGDOM

Showcasing the wonders of Belgian yeast

IV SAISON (SAISON, 6.5% ABV)
BRASSERIE DE JANDRAIN-JANDRENOUILLE
Rue de la Féculerie 34, 1350 Jandrain-Jandrenouille
A dry, characterful Saison produced with four hop varieties, named for the owner's obsession with *Star Wars*.

BT KVEIK (BLONDE ALE, 5.5% ABV)
BREWMINE TAP
Raamstraat 9/bus 1, 3500 Hasselt
An easy-drinking blonde beer with a creamy body (oat flakes) and a tangerine fermentation profile (Norwegian kveik yeast), available to try right next to the brewery in a contemporary city taproom.

FRANÇOIS GRAND CRU
(BELGIAN STRONG GOLDEN ALE, 9% ABV)
BROUWERIJ VARENBROEK
Varenbroekstraat 12, 2840 Rumst
A Tripel fermented with four different types of yeast and dry-hopped with four hop varieties, produced by a lay brewer who for years helped the Cistercians at the Trappist Brouwerij De Achelse Kluis develop and produce their beers.

GOEDENDAG STERK BLOND
(BELGIAN STRONG GOLDEN ALE, 8% ABV)
BROUWERIJ TOYE
Rekkemsestraat, 8510 Marke
A fruity Strong Ale with citrus, bread, and floral notes, named after the brutal 14th-century weapon – a wooden staff combining a club and a spear – used by the militias of medieval Flanders.

HEFE WEISSE NATURTRÜB (HEFEWEIZEN, 5.4% ABV)
BRASSERIE DE LA MULE
Rue Rubens 95, 1030 Schaerbeek
A German-style Hefeweizen with characteristic banana, clove, and bubblegum notes, produced by an ambitious and talented former employee of Brasserie de la Senne as part of his new project in Schaerbeek.

ORVAL VERT (PATERSBIER, 4.5% ABV)
BRASSERIE D'ORVAL
Orval 2, 6823 Villers-devant-Orval
A bitter, fruity, and highly drinkable "Petit Orval" from the brewery at the Abbaye Notre-Dame d'Orval, served only in its famous skittle bottle in the Abbey for the monks and on draught at the nearby café, L'Auberge de L'Ange Gardien (The Guardian Angel Inn).

REMISE TRIPEL (TRIPEL, 8.5% ABV)
REMISE 56
Albert I laan 56, 3582 Beringen
A classic Tripel with a malty, lightly hoppy, and ripe banana character brewed in an impressive old steam tram and bus depot, and showcased best on Duotank draught in the Grand Café on site.

SAISON CAZEAU (SAISON, 5% ABV)
BRASSERIE DE CAZEAU
Rue Cazeau 67, 7520 Tournai
A fruity and floral Saison brewed with Sterling hops and elderflowers, created by a brewer and politician who now serves in the Walloon Parliament.

WINXXXEL (TRIPEL, 9% ABV)
BROUWERIJ ADEPT
Warotstraat 4, 3020 Winksele
A medium-bodied Tripel with notes of mango, banana, and citrus, produced in De Smederij, a cooperative company located in the workshop and house of the town's former blacksmith.

WITTE POL (WITBIER, 5.8% ABV)
BRASSERIE INTER-POL
Mont 34A, 6661 Houffalize
A hazy Witbier with a touch of lemon acidity from a brewer who was once a Flemish language guide at nearby Brasserie d'Achouffe before setting up his own nanobrewery, café, and bed-and-breakfast.

CEREAL KILLERS

Malt and grain to assassinate your cravings

ARMOUT MACLEOD SCOTCH
(BELGIAN SCOTCH ALE, 8.4% ABV)
STADSBROUWERIJ BRAUW
Molenstraat 37/1, 3600 Genk
A beer with liquorice, coffee, and caramel notes, whose name was inspired by Armand Maclot: an artist with Scottish family roots who established a school of painting in Genk in the early 20th century.

BARENTSZ WINTER (QUADRUPEL, 9.2% ABV)
RIMOR BREWERY
Herkveldstraat 36, 3631 Maasmechelen
A Quadrupel from a Flemish newcomer, presenting with a robust roasted and caramel malt character, balanced with dried-fruit fermentation notes, and the addition of passionflower and Ceylon cinnamon.

COURANT (DUBBEL, 6% ABV)
BROUWCOMPAGNIE ROLLING HILLS
Industriepark de Bruwaan 45S, 9700 Oudenaarde
A beer inspired by the dark raw wheat additions of the Courant Oudenaards style from the 1930s, produced by three brothers trying to resurrect a family brewing heritage.

GOUDEN CAROLUS CUVÉE VAN DE KEIZER
(BELGIAN STRONG DARK ALE, 11% ABV)
HET ANKER
Guido Gezellelaan 49, 2800 Mechelen
A beer showcasing the full complexity of the style's caramel, plum, and spice notes, produced by the city brewery once a year to celebrate the birthday of Mechelen's own Emperor Charles V.

IMPERIAL STOUT (RUSSIAN IMPERIAL STOUT, 10% ABV)
BROUWERIJ BROERS
Schoolstraat 7, 9185 Wachtebeke
A big, creamy, chocolatey Imperial Stout from three brothers-in-law who started brewing in their garage but are now moving production to a former church.

LUPULUS HIBERNATUS (WINTER ALE, 9.5% ABV)
BRASSERIE LUPULUS
Courtil 50, 6671 Gouvy
A rich Walloon winter beer from one of the fathers of the Chouffe brand, presenting with a spicy cinnamon finish and brewed with flaked torrefied barley for a stable head and big body.

NOSTRADAMUS (BELGIAN STRONG DARK ALE, 10.2% ABV)
BRASSERIE CARACOLE
Côte Marie-Thérèse 86, 5500 Falmignoul
A Strong Ale with notes of mocha, liquorice, and aniseed, produced by a brewery located in a characterful old building and known for heating water with a wood-fired oven and adorning its beers with images of snails.

PANNEPOT (BELGIAN STRONG DARK ALE, 10% ABV)
DE STRUISE BROUWERS
Kasteelstraat 50, 8640 Vleteren
The luscious, toasty, and sweet flagship beer of the "Sturdy Brewers" – whose punny name and logo also reference a nearby ostrich farm – is named for the dangerous fishing trawlers of the Belgian coast which have claimed many lives.

QANTELAAR (BELGIAN STRONG DARK ALE, 8% ABV)
BROUWERIJ D'OUDE MAALDERIJ
Ardooisestraat 130, 8870 Izegem
A full-bodied ale brewed with five different malts (plus candi sugar), produced by a rockabilly brewer in his eclectic brewpub featuring vintage pinball machines.

TRANSFO BIER (AMERICAN AMBER ALE, 6.4% ABV)
DE CIRCUS BROUWERIJ
Transfostraat 28, 8550 Zwevegem
A hoppy, hazy, amber-coloured ale produced on the same street as the former Transfo power station in Zwevegem by a group of circus performers turned brewers.

UNUSUAL SUSPECTS

Out-of-the ordinary ingredients or processes

BLOEDAPPELSIEN GEUZE
(BLOOD ORANGE LAMBIC, 6.3% ABV)
PUBLITASTING
Paul Wielemansstraat 15, 8570 Anzegem
An acidic, funky blend of Lambics from De Troch, Het Boerenerf, and Den Herberg which has been macerated with blood orange by a new blender of small batches.

BLOOD HONEY SEX MAGIK (MEAD, 14% ABV)
DE MEDERIE
Rue du Petit Marais 16, 7760 Celles
A mead rather than a beer, this barrel-aged ferment of raw sunflower honey, blackcurrants, and raspberries is a berry-forward, slightly acidic creation from an experienced brewer of Pale Ales and Oud Bruins who loves the Red Hot Chilli Peppers.

BOUNTY ISLANDS (COCONUT IMPERIAL STOUT, 10.5% ABV)
BRASSERIE ZYTHOLOGIST
Rue de la Station 30, 6181 Courcelles
A boozy, sweet Imperial Stout aged in rum barrels with the addition of coconut, produced by brewers who like colourful shirts and pastry styles.

JOSEPH (SPELT ALE, 4.5% ABV)
BRASSERIE DE SILENRIEUX
Rue Nou Pré 1, 5630 Cerfontaine
A cloudy ale with notes of citrus and honey brewed with spelt, the "poor man's wheat," produced by a brewery which has been championing alternative cereals and organic beers since the early 1990s.

ONGEDORST (FARMHOUSE ALE, 6.5% ABV)
ANTIDOOT WILDE FERMENTEN
Diestsestraat 41, 3470 Kortenaken
An expressive mixed-fermentation beer with citrusy and woody notes, brewed with raw wheat, raw unhusked spelt, and raw unhusked oats by a former philosophy professor in his home farm brewery.

PUMPKIN'S NIGHTMARE (SPICED PUMPKIN ALE, 7.6% ABV)
MALCROYS BREWING
Albertlei 43, 2550 Kontich
A classic Pumpkin Ale spiced with cinnamon, nutmeg, ginger, and vanilla, and matured on toasted oak chips from bourbon and rum barrels.

ROSEMARY FIELDS FOREVER (LAMBIC BLEND, 6% ABV)
PELLICLE VERGISTINGEN
Sint-Arnolduslaan 72, 8200 Sint-Michiels
A blend of different Lambics macerated on sour Gorsem cherries and fresh rosemary from an up-and-coming West Flemish producer of minimal-intervention beer, cider, and wine.

SPECULOOS STOUT (IMPERIAL COFFEE STOUT, 13% ABV)
TOTEM
Reibroekstraat 101, 9940 Evergem
A full-on Imperial Stout with notes of coffee and a subtle hint of sweet speculoos biscuits, made by an experimental brewery that's been influential in the Ghent beer scene for a decade.

STEENUILKE (HERBED PALE ALE, 6.5% ABV)
BROUWERIJ DE RYCK
Kerkstraat 24, 9550 Herzele
A herbal, fruity, slightly grassy Pale Ale, produced originally to help protect an owl species in the Flemish Ardennes and brewed with three herbs native to its habitat: sweet woodruff, angelica, and blackthorn.

YAK (NORWEGIAN FARMHOUSE ALE WITH SICHUAN PEPPERCORNS, 7% ABV)
STROOM
Forelstraat 27, 9000 Ghent
A citrusy and spicy Farmhouse Ale from an exciting Belgo-American producer in Ghent, named for a giant-battling character from medieval folklore and brewed with the addition of Norwegian kveik yeast and Sichuan peppercorns for an extra kick.

ACKNOWLEDGEMENTS

Thanks to all those who so generously gave their time to speak with us over the years, and who trusted us to tell their stories and showcase them in our photography.

We owe a special thanks to all the staff at Luster Publishing, and particularly to Marc Verhagen and Dettie Luyten, for believing in this project from the beginning and affording us the time and space to deliver the best version we could. We are eternally grateful to Sarah Schrauwen and Mathieu Vancamp of doublebill.design for their work in making this book more beautiful than we could have imagined.

Ashley would like to thank everyone who helped make the photographs in this book possible, and especially her photography assistants Piers Eyre-Walker, Jenna Boheme, Tom Gallo, and Cliff Lucas for following her around Belgium with such patience and enthusiasm.

Ashley would also like to acknowledge Grandpa Sam, the original photographer of the family, who was never without a camera in hand and who inspired her to start shooting with his memorable sayings: "Two Flashes." Ashley is grateful to her parents, AnnJoan and David Hyman, for always supporting her adventurous and creative ideas, even when it means living on opposite sides of the world.

Ashley also thanks Chris Eyre-Walker, for supporting and assisting with the product photography in this book, and for being the reason she was able to discover this special place, its people, and its beer culture.

Breandán would like to thank all those who helped shape the manuscript: Louise Vanderputte for the clarity she brought to the project; Oisín Kearney for his story consultancy and enduring patience; Claire Bullen for her professional rigour and editorial expertise; Katya Doms for her fact-checking diligence and meticulous attention-to-detail; and Eoghan Walsh for his knowhow, creative flair, and friendship.

Breandán is eternally grateful to Rob Tod for doing him the honour of contributing the foreword to this book.

Breandán would also like to thank his parents, Paul Kearney and Eilís Fitzpatrick, for their unconditional love and unwavering support, no matter the direction he's gone in. Breandán is also thankful to his children, Fionn and Oisín, his beloved *Na Fianna van Heule*, who in their short lives have so far taught him more about creative curiosity than a decade of work as a professional writer.

Last, but by no means least, Breandán expresses his gratitude to his wife, Elisa Depypere, who not only introduced him to Belgium and its beer, but who lifts him up every day with her love, kindness, courage, and strength.

GLOSSARY

ABBEY-STYLE ALES

Ales made in the style of beers commonly produced in the Trappist abbeys of Belgium, including styles such as Paterbiers, Tripels, Dubbels, and Quadrupels (Belgian Dark Strong Ales). Most Trappist breweries produce abbey-style ales, but abbey-style ales are not necessarily Trappist beers.

ABV

Alcohol by volume, a standard measure of how much alcohol is contained in a given volume of an alcoholic beverage (expressed as a volume percent).

ALE

A broad class of beers brewed using the top-fermenting ale yeast Saccharomyces cerevisiae, often fermenting quickly and at high temperatures (15–24°C, or 60–78°F). These fermentations yield beers with more fruity, complex flavour profiles. This is in contrast to lower-temperature lager fermentations with Saccharomyces pastorianus or Saccharomyces carlsbergensis yeast, which yield beers with cleaner, more directly ingredient-driven flavour profiles.

ATTENUATION

The conversion of sugars into alcohol and carbon dioxide by the fermentation process; the greater the attenuation, the more sugar has been converted into alcohol. A more attenuated beer is drier and more alcoholic than a less attenuated beer made from the same wort.

BAUDELOT COOLER

A liquid cooler devised by French engineer Jean Louis Baudelot (1797–1881), who studied engineering in Belgium. It's used to cool wort by allowing the hot liquid to run down the outside of its copper tubes into a shallow tray while sending very cool liquid through the insides of the tubes. In this way, cooling takes place more quickly than in a coolship, limiting exposure to contaminating microbes.

BITTERING ADDITION

The hops added at the beginning of the boil, which over the time they're in contact with the hot wort impart bitterness but little aroma.

BRETTANOMYCES / BRETT / WILD BRETTANOMYCES STRAIN

A genus of yeast historically considered a "wild yeast" because of its spoilage capabilities and the characteristically funky flavours and aromas it can produce. It is traditionally associated with old Stock Ale from 19th-century Britain (its name means "British fungus") and it is recognised for its presence in Lambics and other spontaneous and mixed-fermentation beers in Belgium.

CARBONATION

The presence of carbon dioxide gas in a liquid. The effects of carbonation strongly influence a beer's mouthfeel, flavour, aroma, and appearance. Carbon dioxide gas is produced naturally during fermentation and is readily soluble in the beer. Brewers can also inject finished beer with carbon dioxide to their desired levels in what is often described as "forced carbonation."

CENTRIFUGATION

The application of radial forces upon wort or beer by moving it in a circular motion at high speeds. The liquid is laden with various types of suspended particulate, including yeast, trub, and hop residue, each with a different density. Applying centrifugal forces helps separate out the heaviest particles from the lighter ones, and clarifies the wort or beer.

CLEAN FERMENTATIONS

Fermentations involving a pure-culture yeast strain as opposed to "wild" processes involving complex and more unpredictable fermentations.

COLLOIDAL DROP-OUT

The process whereby substances suspended within beer – generally protein molecules and polyphenols – sediment to the bottom of the vessel.

CONDITIONING

The achievement, post-fermentation, of a particular beer's correct character of maturation and carbonation. As such, "conditioning" is a catchall term that may include lagering, relatively warm ageing in a tank, refermentation in the bottle, or refermentation in a cask. During conditioning, yeast "cleans up" unwanted flavour compounds such as diacetyl (butter or popcorn) and acetaldehyde (green apple).

CONTRACT FACILITY

A brewery where contract brewing takes place. Contract brewing is an arrangement in which a beer company pays another brewery to produce its beer, not to be confused with cuckoo brewing.

COOLSHIP INOCULATION

The often-passive introduction of yeast or bacteria microbes into a beer in a coolship (in Flemish, *koelschip*), a broad, open-top, flat vessel in which wort cools.

CUBITAINERS

Plastic cube-shaped containers inside heavy-duty corrugated outer frames, convenient for the shipping and storage of liquids such as wort, beer, and brewing chemicals.

CUCKOO BREWERS

Brewers who don't have their own equipment but use that of another brewery. Whereas beer companies contracting their beers at contract facilities will supply a recipe that the contract facility produces, cuckoo brewers physically brew their beers themselves at different breweries.

CUVEÉ

A term deriving from French wine culture (*cuve* means vat or tank), used in Belgian beer most often to denote a special beer of higher quality in comparison to the producer's regular offerings.

DECOCTION MASHING

A method of mashing that raises the temperature of the mash by removing a portion, boiling it, and returning it to the mash tun. This method is often used multiple times in a single brew. Many brewers claim that it develops malt character, depth, and superior foam.

DIASTATICUS

A variant of Saccharomyces cerevisiae with the ability to modify the fermentability of beer due to a special gene (STA) which causes the organism to secrete glucoamylase (an enzyme which hydrolyzes dextrins and starches into fermentable sugars). As such, this can lead to beers that are drier, stronger, and more highly attenuated. However, these diastatic fermentations can be slow and difficult to detect, and so if this happens after packaging, additional fermentation can lead to over-carbonation and changes in flavour.

DRY-HOP / DRY-HOPPING

The addition of hops late in the brewing process to increase the hop aroma of a finished beer without significantly affecting its bitterness.

DDH

Double dry-hopped: beers that have been dry-hopped twice.

EBC

European Brewing Convention, a scale to measure the colour intensity of a beer. A Pale Lager will generally have an EBC colour of ~4, an Amber Ale ~33, and an Imperial Stout ~138.

ENZYMATIC SACCHARIFICATION

The conversion of cereal starches into sugars and dextrins during the mashing process. This conversion is carried out by enzymes, proteins which bind to starch molecules in the mash and speed up the chemical reactions required to break them down to sugars.

ESTERS

Flavour compounds that produce the "fruity" aromas in beer (not including the direct addition of fruit and fruit flavours in certain beers). Esters are formed by the reactions of organic acids and alcohols created during fermentation. The most significant esters found in Belgian beer are isoamyl acetate (banana, peardrop), ethyl acetate (fruit, solvent), ethyl caprylate (apple), ethyl hexanoate (apple, aniseed), and phenylethyl acetate (rose, honey).

FERMENTABLES

Any substance that can be fermented. In brewing, fermentables are the sugars yeast digest to make alcohol. These most often derive from grain, but can come from other sources of sugar.

FERMENTATION

The process whereby sugars are converted by yeast to alcohol, carbon dioxide, and heat. In the brewing of most traditional beer, the sugars are derived mainly from malted barley, although other cereal sources and plant sugars can also be used. These materials also contribute proteins, which together with the sugars and added flavouring agents, notably hops, generate the alcohol, flavours, and aromas of beer.

FILTRATION

The process of removing suspended particles from beer; the separation of solids from liquids by passage through a filter. Filtration helps stabilise beer and give it a polished, clear appearance, but some brewers prefer not to filter as they argue essential flavour compounds and proteins may be lost.

FOEDER

A large vertical or horizontal oak barrel where beer – most often wild and sour beer – can be aged or fermented.

GRAIN BASE

Sometimes referred to as a "grain bill," "grist bill," or "mash bill," this is the list of cereals in a recipe that brewers use to produce the wort that they then ferment into alcohol.

HECTOLITRE(S)

A metric unit of capacity equal to 100 litres, used especially for beer and wine.

HOP EXTRACTS

Products developed from the extraction of the hop components that are important to brewers, such as the alpha acids and essential oils that contribute bitterness, aroma, head retention, and stability. Hop extracts eliminate much of the inert biological materials that come with using hop pellets or whole-leaf hops, meaning less trub in the bottom of the brew kettle.

HOUSE CULTURE / HOUSE YEAST

A yeast strain or mixed culture used by a brewery for most or all of its beers. It can be propagated from another brewery's culture, the result of a blend, "captured" in nature, or purchased commercial yeast.

IBU

International Bitterness Units, a scale to gauge the level of a beer's bitterness. IBUs measure the parts per million of hop isohumulone in beer. For example: An American Light Lager generally has a bitterness range of 8-12 IBUs; an English Bitter 25-35 IBUs; and an American IPA 40-70 IBUs.

LACTOBACILLUS

Often referred to by brewers as "Lacto," a genus of lactic acid bacteria that produces acidity and sour flavours in the form of lactic acid and secondary metabolites. It's often used to ferment Lambics, Berliner Weisses, Oud Bruins, and Geuzes.

LAGER

A beer that is brewed at cool temperatures (7–13°C, or 45–55°F) by fermenting with a slow-acting yeast (typically Saccharomyces pastorianus or Saccharomyces carlsbergensis). Lagers include Bocks, Pilsners, and Schwarzbiers, among other styles. The lower-temperature fermentation yields beers with cleaner, more directly ingredient-driven flavour profiles than those fermented at higher temperatures with Saccharomyces cerevisiae. The term "lager" comes from the German word for "storage."

LAGERING

Storing beer at cold temperatures during a period of ageing and conditioning, sometimes accompanied by a secondary fermentation to improve flavour and clarity.

LAMBIC

Spontaneously fermented wheat beer, most often brewed in Brussels and the Pajottenland, and aged in oak barrels or foeders. Lambics are made using complex fermentations based on locally and naturally occurring wild yeasts and bacteria. They can be blended to become Geuzes, aged on fruit such as *krieken* (cherries), or sweetened to become Faro.

MACERATION

A process that involves soaking (or steeping) raw agricultural ingredients in liquid, which softens them and draws out their natural juices. It is a technique that is most used in Belgian brewing to enhance and extract the flavours of fruit.

MALT

Processed grain which has been modified for use in brewing from its natural state by a multistep procedure called malting, which involves being steeped, germinated, dried, and kilned.

MASHING

The process of mixing milled grains – typically malted barley with supplemental grains such as corn, sorghum, rye, or wheat – with water and then heating the mixture. Mashing allows the enzymes in the malt to break down the starch in the grain into sugars, which can then be fermented.

MASH SCHEME

The steps taken when mashing, including the time and temperature at each particular step. Different mashing times and temperatures will affect the ways enzymes break down grain starch into sugars, and will impact the dryness and mouthfeel of a beer.

MASH CONVERSION

The process by which starch in the brewing grain is converted into sugars which can be used by yeast in fermentation.

MIXED FERMENTATION / MIXED-CULTURE FERMENTATION

A multi-species mixed fermentation consists of a combination of Saccharomyces (brewer's yeast), Brettanomyces (wild yeast), Lactobacillus (lactic acid bacteria), and Pediococcus (lactic acid bacteria), or other microbes that are unconventional in brewing. These beers often have complex flavour and aroma profiles.

HUMULUS NEOMEXICANUS

A genetically distinct subspecies of hop plant that has been growing in the American Southwest for thousands of years. Neomexicanus hop varieties are characterful, high-efficiency, and drought-resistant.

OUD BRUIN

A style of mixed-fermentation beer traditionally produced in Flanders, typically with a sweet and sour flavour profile and often involving long maturation and blending. Some draw distinctions between stainless steel-matured Oud Bruin from the Oudenaarde region and oak foeder- or barrel-matured Flanders Red from southwestern Flanders, but Oud Bruin is the most commonly used term for all types of Flemish red-brown mixed-fermentation beer which is aged.

PASTEURISATION

The process of heating beer to a temperature that will kill any living microbes. It is used by some brewers to sterilise and stabilise their product, without changing the chemistry. Some brewers argue that rapid heating and chilling diminishes the flavour and aroma of the beer.

PHENOLICS

A broad class of polyphenol compounds responsible for many well-known flavours and aromas in Belgian beer, such as clove and pepper, but sometimes showing up as undesirable off-flavours when they present as plastic, smoke, medicinal, or Band-Aid.

PILSNER

A pale, golden lager, originally from the Czech Republic.

PITCH

Adding yeast to wort.

PRIMARY FERMENTATION

The first stage of fermentation, beginning as soon as yeast inoculates the wort. (Secondary fermentation is a somewhat catch-all term referring to any phase of fermentation following the very active primary fermentation, but before complete removal of the yeast.)

PURE-CULTURE YEAST

A laboratory culture containing a single species of yeast, used by brewers for its defined profile and predictability.

REFERMENTATION

The process by which a small amount of yeast is added to a beer just before packaging. In Belgium, this is often at the bottling stage and known as bottle conditioning or bottle refermentation.

SACCHAROMYCES CEREVISIAE / SACCHAROMYCES ALE YEAST

Top-fermenting ale yeast, often referred to as "brewer's yeast." Saccharomyces is a Latin term meaning "sugar fungus." Cerevisiae means "of beer."

SHELF STABILITY

The extent to which a beer will stay in a desirable and stable state in shops, bars, restaurants, etc.

SPÉCIALE BELGE

An amber-coloured Belgian ale with a subtle maltiness, a fruity fermentation profile, and a slightly bitter aftertaste.

SPONTANEOUS FERMENTATION

The inoculation of wort by whichever organisms (yeast and bacteria) happen to be in the air or in the environment in which the wort is being cooled after brewing.

TANNIC

A quality deriving from tannins, a group of organic compounds contained in certain cereal grains, other plants such as hops, and also found in many types of wood. Tannic quality in beer can be perceived as a furry, drying, or even astringent sensation on the palate.

TOP FERMENTATION

A mode of fermentation generally associated with ales, in which flocculating yeast rises to the surface of the fermenting wort, rendering it possible to "skim" the crop of yeast from the surface of the vessel and make it ready for transfer to the next batch of wort. (In "bottom fermentation," the yeast, typically a lager yeast variety, drops to the bottom of the fermentation vessel.)

TRAPPISTS

Relating to or denoting a branch of the Cistercian order of monks founded in 1664 and noted for austere rules that include remaining silent for much of the time. At the time of publication, there are five breweries in Belgium that produce beer with the Authentic Trappist Product logo.

TRUB

Coming from the German word for "sediment," a collective term covering proteins, hop oils, tannins, and other particles that precipitate during the boiling and cooling stages of brewing.

WHIRLPOOL AROMA ADDITION

A brewing technique where hops are added to the whirlpool vessel after the boil, helping extract hop flavour and aroma without contributing excessive bitterness.

WORT

The liquid extracted from the mashing process during the brewing of beer. Wort contains malt-derived sugars that will be fermented by the brewing yeast to produce alcohol. Wort also contains crucial amino acids to provide nitrogen to the yeast as well as more complex proteins contributing to beer head retention and flavour.

NOTES

I've compiled notes about my reporting sources, including interviews, historical texts, books, magazines, videos, articles, and other references. Interviews listed include subsequent personal email and text communications.

GENERAL: BOOKS

Daniels, Ray; and Mosher, Randy. *Tasting Beer, 2nd Edition: An Insider's Guide to the World's Greatest Drink.* Storey Publishing, LLC, 2017.

De Baets, Yvan; and Stange, Joe. *Around Brussels in 80 Beers.* Cogan & Mater, 2009.

De Raedemaeker, Luc; and Verdonck, Erik. *The Belgian Beer Book.* Lannoo Publishers, 2024.

Deweer, Hilde, and Van Damme, Jaak. *All Belgian Beers.* Stichting Kunstboek, 2015.

Gatz, Sven. *De Vier Seizoenen van Het Belgisch Bier.* Uitgeverij van Halewyck, 2012.

Guinard, Jean. *Lambic (Classic Beer Style Series).* Brewers Publications, 1998.

Hieronymus, Stan. *Brew Like a Monk: Trappist, Abbey, and Strong Belgian Ales and How to Brew Them.* Brewers Publications, 2005.

Hieronymus, Stan. *Brewing with Wheat: The "Wit" and "Weizen" of Wheat Beer Styles.* Brewers Publications, 2010.

Jackson, Michael. *Great Beers of Belgium.* Brewers Publications, 2008.

Lefebvre, Sylvie; Symons, Thérèse; and van Praag, Yannick. *Estaminets and Cafés: Brussels Stories: Collective Work.* BruxellesFabriques = Brusselfabriek, 2018.

Markowski, Phil. *Farmhouse Ales: Culture and Craftsmanship in the Belgian Tradition.* Brewers Publications, 2004.

Meert, Raf. *Lambic: The Untamed Brussels Beer: Origin, Evolution and Future.* Serendippo, 2022.

Oliver, Garrett, editor. *The Oxford Companion to Beer.* Oxford University Press, 2011.

Querci, Niccolò. *Brussels: The Beer Capital: Beer Guide to the City.* Independently Published, 2023.

Rajotte, Pierre. *Belgian Ale (Classic Beer Style Series).* Brewers Publications, 1998.

Roncoroni, Miguel, and Verstrepen, Kevin. *Belgian Beer: Tested and Tasted.* Lannoo Publishers, 2018.

Scholliers, Peter. *Food Culture in Belgium.* Greenwood Press, 2009.

Sparrow, Jeff. *Wild Brews: Beer Beyond the Influence of Brewer's Yeast.* Brewers Publications, 2005.

Stange, Joe; and Webb, Tim. *CAMRA's Good Beer Guide Belgium.* 8th ed., Campaign for Real Ale, 2018.

Van den Steen, Jef. *Belgian Trappist and Abbey Beers: Truly Divine.* Lannoo Publishers, 2018.

Walsh, Eoghan. *A History of Brussels Beer in 50 Objects.* Independently Published, 2022.

Walsh, Eoghan. *Brussels Beer City: Stories from Brussels' Brewing Past.* Independently Published, 2020.

Ysewijn, Regula. *Belgian Cafe Culture.* Luster Publishing, 2021.

GENERAL: ONLINE RESOURCES

"BJCP Style Guidelines." Beer Judge Certification Program, *www.bjcp.org/bjcp-style-guidelines*.

CraftBeer.Com, *www.craftbeer.com*.

GENERAL: MAGAZINES

Belgian Beer and Food Magazine, no. 1–18.

Bier Grand Cru.

Bierpassie Magazine.

Craft Beer & Brewing.

PASSE-PARTOUT

De Bont, Frans. Personal interview by Oisín Kearney. 12 June 2022. Conducted in Baarle-Hertog.

Koops, Enne. "De Dodendraad – Dodelijke Draadversperring Tijdens de Eerste Wereldoorlog." *Historiek*, 9 Nov. 2023.

Mengerink, Ronald. Personal interview. 7 Mar. 2018. Conducted at Brouwerij De Dochter van de Korenaar, Oordeelstraat 3B, 2387 Baarle-Hertog.

Mengerink, Ronald. Personal interviews. 16 Dec. 2022, 18 Jan. 2023, and 16 Aug. 2023. Conducted remotely.

Van Gool, Willem. Personal interview by Oisín Kearney. 12 June 2022. Conducted in Baarle-Hertog.

SPACE CADET

Bauweraerts, Chris; Boon, Frank; Mattheus, Miel; Perkins, Jason; and Tod, Rob. Personal interview. 9 Nov. 2022. Conducted at Ma Façon, Altenaken 11a, 3320 Hoegaarden.

Delvaux, Filip. *Haze: A Determining Factor in White Beers, Diss. Katholieke Universiteit Leuven*, Katholieke Universiteit, 2001.

Hieronymus, Stan. "Chapter Three: In Search of the Real Belgian White Ale." *Brewing with Wheat: The "Wit" and "Weizen" of World Wheat Beer Styles*, Brewers Publications, 2010, pp. 37–69.

Lippens, Alex; Tack, Jens; and Van Lancker, Koen. Personal interviews. 8 June 2016, 2 Aug. 2017, 4 Jan. 2018, and 17 Oct. 2023. Conducted at Brouwerij 't Verzet, Grote Leiestraat 117, 8570 Anzegem.

Poelmans, Eline, and Swinnen, Johan F. M. "1 A Brief Economic History of Beer." *The Economics of Beer*, 1 Oct. 2011, pp. 3–28, https://doi.org/10.1093/acprof:oso/9780199693801.003.0001.

COLLEKE

Delvaux, Bart; and Van der Stock, Ine. Personal interview. 13 July 2022. Conducted at Brouwerij de Coureur, Borstelsstraat 20/bus 1, 3010 Leuven.

Marshall, Jeremy. "Definition of Cream Ale." *The Oxford Companion to Beer | Craft Beer & Brewing*, beerandbrewing.com/dictionary/fHr9zWIBTS.

PILS 13 DELTA

Brown, Pete. "Definition of Pilsner." *The Oxford Companion to Beer | Craft Beer & Brewing*, beerandbrewing.com/dictionary/ViBLMl59ag/.

"Czech Lager." *Beer Judge Certification Program*, www.bjcp.org/style/2021/3.

De Baets, Janos. Personal interview. 29 Nov. 2021. Conducted at Dok Brewing Company, Dok-Noord 4B, 9000 Ghent.

"International Lager." *Beer Judge Certification Program*, www.bjcp.org/style/2021/2.

Messiaen, Dimitri. Personal interview. 23 Aug. 2023. Conducted at Messiaen's home in Sint-Amandsberg.

"Pale Bitter European Beer." *Beer Judge Certification Program*, www.bjcp.org/style/2021/5.

GUEUZE HET BOERENERF

De Keersmaeker, Erik. Personal interview. 18 Jan. 2024. Conducted remotely.

Delplancq, Thierry. "Les Brasseries de Lambic. Données Historiques et Géographiques (XVIIIe-XXe) (1)." *Archives et Bibliothèques de Belgique.*, 1996.

Eylenbosch, Senne. Personal interview. 14 Nov. 2022. Conducted at Het Boerenerf, Sollenberg 3, 1654 Beersel.

"Sollenberg." *Sollenberg | Inventaris Onroerend Erfgoed*, id.erfgoed.net/themas/17136.

Blancquaert, Michaël; and Van Obberghen, Werner. 2023. Personal email communications.

OUDE QUETSCHE TILQUIN À L'ANCIENNE

"Horal Website (Hoge Raad Voor Ambachtelijke Lambiekbieren)." *High Council for Traditional Lambic Beers*, 27 Nov. 2023, www.horal.be.

Tilquin, Pierre. Personal interview. 30 Apr. 2016. Conducted at Gueuzerie Tilquin, Chaussée Maïeur Habils 110, 1430 Bierghes (Rebecq).

Tilquin, Pierre. Personal interview. 30 Mar. 2019. Conducted in Ghent.

Tilquin, Pierre. Personal interview. 1 May 2021. Conducted at Café In de Verzekering tegen de Grote Dorst, Frans Baetensstraat 45, 1750 Eizeringen (Lennik).

Tilquin, Pierre. Personal interview. 18 Sep. 2023. Conducted remotely.

BIZON

Cnudde, Lander; and Cnudde, Lieven. Personal interview. 6 Apr. 2021. Conducted at Brouwerij Cnudde, Fabrieksstraat 8, 9700 Oudenaarde.

Delrue, Karel-Willem. *Brouwerij Cnudde: 100 Jaar Brouwkunst 1919–2019*. Boekhandel Beatrijs, 2019.

Delrue, Karel-Willem. Personal interview. 16 Feb. 2021. Conducted remotely.

De Waele, Chris. Personal interview. 15 Apr. 2021. Conducted remotely.

Pipik, Jane. "A World War I Hero's Family Found His Story Alive and Well in Belgium." *The World from PRX*, 11 Nov. 2014, theworld.org/stories/2014-11-11/world-war-i-heros-family-found-his-story-alive-and-well-belgium.

CUVÉE FREDDY

Castelein, Glenn; De Keukeleire, Marc; and Murgioni, Ricardo. Personal interview. 21 Aug. 2023. Conducted at Brouwerij Alvinne, Vaartstraat 4a, 8552 Moen.

Castelein, Glenn. Personal interview. 2 May 2018. Conducted at The Oval Space, 29–32 The Oval, Cambridge Heath, London E2 9DT, UK.

Willams, Bethany. "Morpheus: The Greek God of Dreams and Nightmares." *The Collector*, 18 Mar. 2022, www.thecollector.com/morpheus-greek-god.

HARZINGTON

Gould, Kenny. "How the Alchemist Goes Above and Beyond to Give You Sustainable Beer." *Forbes*, Forbes Magazine, 10 Jan. 2020, www.forbes.com/sites/kennygould/2020/01/09/how-the-alchemist-goes-above-and-beyond-to-give-you-sustainable-beer/?sh=3b700454e703.

Kimmich, John. 2023. Personal email communications.

Patsalides, Samia; and Perée, Rémy. Personal interview. 7 Sep. 2022. Conducted at Misery Beer Co., Pouhon 22, 4920 Harzé.

Torfs, Michaël. "90 Percent of Walloon Municipalities Hit by the Floods, Death Toll Is Still Rising." *Vrtnws.Be*, VRT NWS: news, 18 July 2021, *www.vrt.be/vrtnws/en/2021/07/18/from-railroads-to-tap-water-the-impact-of-the-floods-is-huge*.

KEIKOPPENBIER

Cambie, Joris. Personal interviews. 30 Aug. 2014 and 18 Jan. 2017. Conducted at Brouwerij De Plukker, Elverdingseweg 14A, 8970 Poperinge.

Cambie, Joris. Personal interview. 21 June 2016. Conducted in Ghent.

Cambie, Joris. Personal interviews. 15 Aug. 2022 and 18 Jan. 2024. Conducted remotely.

Langouche, Kris. 2023-2024. Personal email communications.

Van der Bauwhede, Valerie. Personal interview. 20 Jan. 2024. Conducted at Terrest Brewery, Vlastraat 1, 8650 Houthulst.

ELDORADO

"El Dorado® Hops: Freedom for Your Beer." El Dorado, *www.eldoradohops.com*.

Larsimont, Jean-Christophe. Personal interview. 6 Sep. 2022. Conducted at Brasserie De La Sambre / Brasserie Des Champs, Rue de la Tour, 5190 Spy (Jemeppe-sur-Sambre).

VALEIR EXTRA

De Vrieze, Frederik. Personal interview. 14 Jan. 2016. Conducted at Brouwerij Contreras, Molenstraat 110, 9890 Gavere.

De Vrieze, Frederik. Personal interviews. 9 Dec. 2022 and 12 Dec. 2022. Conducted remotely.

"Tour of Flanders." Flanders Classics Events, *www.rondevanvlaanderen.be/en*.

Vandewalle, Thomas. "Brouwerij Contreras Bestaat 200 Jaar." *HLN.Be*, DPG Media, 2 Aug. 2018, *www.hln.be/gavere/brouwerij-contreras-bestaat-200-jaar~a7e09a21*.

BIÈRE DE TABLE

Boorman, John, director. *Deliverance*. Warner Bros., 1972.

Bravin, Christophe; and Damien, Félix. Personal interview. 2 Aug. 2023. Conducted at Brasserie La Jungle, Rue de la Petite Île 1A, 1070 Anderlecht.

Noire, Guillaume. 2023. Personal email communications.

Pirenne, Martin. 2023. Personal email communications.

CUVÉE DEVILLÉ

Devillé, Bart; and Devillé, Kloris. Personal interview. 15 Aug. 2018. Conducted at Brouwerij Den Herberg, Octave de Kerchove d'Exaerdestraat 16, 1501 Halle.

Devillé, Kloris. Personal interview. 11 Jan. 2023. Conducted remotely.

LA MONEUSE

Carlier, Kévin; and Pourtois, Marie-Noëlle. Personal interview. 6 Feb. 2023. Conducted at Brasserie de Blaugies, Rue de la Frontière 435, 7370 Dour.

Carlier, Pierre-Alex. Personal interview. 23 Aug. 2018. Conducted at Brasserie de Blaugies, Rue de la Frontière 435, 7370 Dour.

DiPietro, Sandro. "Quartiers d'histoires: Joseph-Antoine Moneuse, Un Brigand de Légende." *Tele MB*, 17 Jan. 2020, *www.telemb.be/emission/archives/quartiers-dhistoires-joseph-antoine-moneuse-un-brigand-de-legende/25789*.

"Généalogie de Antoine-Joseph - Le Bandit." *Geneanet*, gw.geneanet.org/danielmonneuse?lang=fr&n=monneuse&p=antoine%2Bjoseph.

Jottrand, Albert. *Moneuse: Un Chef de Bandits Sous Le Directoire*. E. Bruylant; Mons et Frameries, Union Des Imprimeries S.A, 1944.

Vasseur, Yves. *Antoine-Joseph Moneuse Aventure de Paille et d'ortie: Récit*. Illustrated by Renard, Claude. La Voix Dans Les Saules, 1987.

ARDENNE SAISON

Cleeremans, Marc. Personal interview. 18 Oct. 2023. Conducted at Brasserie Minne, Zone d'Activités Nord 9, 5377 Somme-Leuze.

Minne, Philippe; and Minne-Vanderwauwen, Catherine. Personal interview. 18 Oct. 2023. Conducted at Brasserie Minne, Zone d'Activités Nord 9, 5377 Somme-Leuze.

"Pukkelpop 1995." *Pukkelpop 2019*, 2019.pukkelpop.be/en/history/1995.

FRANC BELGE

Bacelle, Nino. Personal interview. 13 Nov. 2015. Conducted at Brasserie De Ranke, Rue du Petit Tourcoing 1a, 7711 Dottignies.

Bacelle, Nino. Personal interview. 19 July 2016. Conducted in Ghent.

Bacelle, Nino. Personal interview. 16 Dec. 2022. Conducted remotely.

"Beer Mat of Brasserie Du Faleau." *LastDodo*, www.lastdodo.com/en/items/9198991-brasserie-du-faleau.

"Franc Belge, Brasserie de Ranke." *FEBED*, Press Release, 1 Feb. 2019, *www.febed.be/fr/nouvelles/franc-belge-brasserie-de-ranke*.

"Letterhead of Brasserie et Malterie Du Faleau, Chatelineau." *Fou de Capsules*, fou-de-capsules.be/en/brewery/?APasser=Faleau.

Vergracht, Tom. "'All about… Speciale Belge' Presented by Tom Vergracht." *EBCU*, European Beer Consumers Union, 26 Feb. 2024, *youtu.be/9svAoSTEfPo?si=tIH9NlOPXHaNASOM&t=937*.

TRIOMF

Daloze, Laurent. Personal interview. 18 Oct. 2023. Conducted at Brasserie Dupont, Rue Basse 5, 7904 Leuze-en-Hainaut.

Dedeycker, Olivier. 2023. Personal email communications.

Lateur, Servaas. "100 Jaar Vooruit." *Amsab-Instituut Voor Sociale Geschiedenis*, TIC – Tijdschrift Voor Industriële Cultuur, 2013, pp. 2–13.

Simons, Gust. 2023-2024. Personal email communications.

Vandewalle, Chris. "45 Jaar Leven in de Brouwerij: De Geschiedenis van Brouwerij Vooruit." *Van Arbeiderspaleis Tot Kunstencentrum 100 Jaar Vooruit*, TIC – Tijdschrift Voor Industriële Cultuur, 2013, pp. 14–24.

Verhoysen, Willie. Personal interview. 15 June 2023. Conducted in the Vooruit Building, Kunstencentrum VIERNULVIER vzw, Sint-Pietersnieuwstraat 23, 9000 Ghent.

SPECIAL EXTRA EXPORT STOUT

"Foreign Extra Stout." *Beer Judge Certification Program*, www.bjcp.org/style/2021/16/16D/foreign-extra-stout.

Herteleer, Kris. Personal interview. 27 May 2016. Conducted at De Dolle Brouwers, Roeselarestraat 12b, 8600 Diksmuide.

Herteleer, Kris. Personal interview. 15 June 2019. Conducted in London.

Herteleer, Kris. Personal interview. 16 Dec. 2022. Conducted remotely.

VICARIS WINTER

Bastiaens, Kristof; and Dilewyns, Claire. Personal interview. 29 June 2023. Conducted at Brouwerij Dilewyns, Vlassenhout 5, Industrieterrein Hoogveld, 9200 Dendermonde.

"Ommegang." *Ros Beiaard Stad Dendermonde*, www.rosbeiaard.be.

WHITE GOLD

"Andermans Zaken." Season 3, Episode 1, 52 Mins, *VRT*, VRT Max, 2024, www.vrt.be/vrtmax/a-z/andermans-zaken/3/andermans-zaken-s3a1.

Cornelis, Yannah. Personal interview. 17 Apr. 2020. Conducted remotely.

Cornelis, Yannah. Personal interview. 8 July 2020. Conducted at Praktijkpunt Landbouw.

Janssens, Jef. Personal interview. 24 May 2015. Conducted at Brouwerij Hof ten Dormaal, Caubergstraat 2, 3150 Tildonk.

Janssens, Jef. Personal interview. 24 May 2015. Conducted at Den Hoorn, Sluisstraat 79, 3000 Leuven.

Janssens, Jef. Personal interview. 15 Aug. 2022. Conducted remotely.

"Janssens' Way (Interview with André Janssens)." *Beer Idiots YouTube Channel*, 11 May 2019, youtu.be/IdkRWYpJfyI?si=HU_p6IOe8HJ01Lk1.

Dockx, Ingrid; and Pasteels, Jan. Personal interview. 5 Aug. 2020. Conducted at the Hof De Soete farm, Drogenbosstraat 3, 3020 Herent.

Taragola, Nicole. "Belgian Endive: From Tradition to Innovation." *52nd Seminar, June 19–21, 1997, Parma, Italy 231419*, European Association of Agricultural Economists, 19 June 1997.

Taragola, Nicole. 2020. Personal email communications.

Vlaams-Brabant, Blauwe Stap 25, 3020 Herent.

THÉORÈME DE L'EMPEREUR

IMDb. "Alejandro Jodorowsky | Writer, Director, Actor." *IMDb*, IMDb.com, www.imdb.com/name/nm0423524.

Bensaria, Henri; Menu, Nacim; and Simon, François. Personal interviews. 16 Mar. 2018 and 17 Oct. 2023. Conducted at Brasserie de l'Ermitage, Rue Lambert Crickx 26, 1070 Anderlecht.

Menu, Nacim. Personal interview. 13 June 2018. Conducted remotely.

Pavich, Frank, director. *Jodorowsky's Dune*. Sony Pictures Classics, 2014.

ADELHEID

Broekx, Steven. Personal interview. 12 May 2021. Conducted remotely.

Vandormael, Geert. Personal interview. 25 May 2021. Conducted remotely.

Tack, Kristof. Personal interview. 27 May 2021. Conducted remotely.

Broekx, Steven; and Vandormael, Geert. Personal interview. 8 May 2024. Conducted remotely.

DE VLIER BRUT

Andries, Marc; and Schuyten, Karen. Personal interview. 20 Oct. 2023. Conducted at Brouwerij De Vlier, Leuvensebaan 219, 3220 Holsbeek.

HIDDEN BEERS OF BELGIUM

Curation and writing
Breandán Kearney

Photography
Ashley Joanna

Additional photography
p. 4: Mat Trogner, courtesy of Allagash Brewing Company
p. 16, 206, 211: Cliff Lucas
p. 149: Chris Eyre-Walker

Editing
Louise Vanderputte
Oisín Kearney
Claire Bullen
Katya Doms

Graphic design
doublebill.design

D/2024/12.005/12
ISBN 9789460583704
NUR 440

© 2024 Luster Publishing, Antwerp
lusterpublishing.com
info@lusterpublishing.com
@lusterbooks

Printed in Italy.

All rights reserved.
No part of this publication may be reproduced,
stored in a retrieval system, or transmitted, in any form
or by any means, without the prior written consent
of the publisher. An exception is made for short excerpts,
which may be cited for the sole purpose of reviews.